D0260408

GLOBAL RESOURCES

XIV Nobel Conference

GLOBAL RESOURCES: PERSPECTIVES AND ALTERNATIVES

edited by

Clair N. McRostie, Ph.D.

Chairman, Department of Economics and Business
Gustavus Adolphus College
St. Peter, Minnesota

With contributions by *Barry Commoner,*
Latitia Obeng, Tjalling Koopmans,
Garrett Hardin, and *Ian Barbour*

University Park Press

Baltimore

UNIVERSITY PARK PRESS
International Publishers in Science, Medicine, and Education
233 East Redwood Street
Baltimore, Maryland 21202

Copyright © 1980 by University Park Press

Composed by University Park Press, Typesetting Division
Manufactured in the United States of America by The Maple Press
Company

All rights, including that of translation into other languages, reserved.
Photomechanical reproduction (photocopy, microcopy) of this book or
parts thereof without special permission of the publisher is prohibited.

Proceedings of the XIVth Nobel Conference, "Global Resources: Perspectives and Alternatives," held at Gustavus Adolphus College, St. Peter, Minnesota, October 3–4, 1978.

Library of Congress Cataloging in Publication Data
Nobel Conference, 14th, Gustavus Adolphus College, 1978.
Global resources.
Includes index.
1. Natural resources—Congresses. I. Commoner, Barry, 1917–
II. McRostie, Clair N. III. Gustavus Adolphus College, St. Peter, Minn.
IV. Title. HC55.N6 1978 333 79-1971
ISBN 0-8391-1523-7

Contents

Contributors

Barry Commoner, Ph.D.
University Professor of
Environmental Science
Washington University
St. Louis, Missouri 63130

Latitia Obeng, Ph.D.
Senior Program Officer
Division of Environmental
Management
United Nations Environmental
Program
Nairobi, Kenya

Garrett Hardin, Ph.D.
Professor of Human Ecology
University of California
at Santa Barbara
Santa Barbara, California
93106

Ian Barbour, Ph.D.
Professor of Religion and
Professor of Physics
Carleton College
Northfield, Minnesota 55057

Tjalling C. Koopmans, Ph.D.
Nobel Laureate
Alfred Cowles Professor of
Economics
Yale University
New Haven, Connecticut
06520

Preface

The world's supply of resources—their adequacy for the short run and for the long run and their distribution—will continue to be one of man's prime concerns. The issues are as personal and immediate as the assurance of safe water supplies for remote villages and as complex as the sources of energy for the world's future generations. The XIVth Nobel Conference, hosted by Gustavus Adolphus College on October 3 and 4, 1978, sought to bridge the gaps, present alternative analyses of the problems, and provide some direction, if not ultimate solutions.

The conference proceedings published in this volume provide the reader with five very different and unique analyses. Dr. Barry Commoner takes the reader through a process of transition from the depletion of nonrenewable sources of energy to the intermediate step of heating systems using natural gas with conversion to methane gas—a solar fuel—produced from organic waste or crops. Dr. Commoner points out that fossil fuels exist in sufficient supply to sustain the transition to solar energy.

Dr. Latitia Obeng presents an almost poetic plea that basic resources be provided for all people. Human life is put in perspective with all natural resources. Human dependance and need are vividly portrayed. Her plea is not only for better resource stewardship and management but also for the assurance of equitable use of resources for the benefit of all mankind. Dr. Obeng challenges society to decide whether satisfactory development of all peoples of the Third and Fourth Worlds and the poor of the First and Second Worlds is a right or charity.

Nobel Laureate Tjalling Koopmans provides the essential economics compliment to the other papers. He emphasizes the calculation and comparison of long-range projections into the future that are arrived at in collaboration with other disciplines. Koopmans modifies the traditional competitive equilibrium model with the consideration of shadow prices of goods and bads that are not traded in the markets. In order to visualize the alternative futures of an economy, Koopmans employs the mathematics of discounting. Koopmans joins Commoner in concern for the development of energy sources as the key to adequacy of resources. Finally, Koopmans reaches beyond the question of resource adequacy to that of diminishing population growth and evolution into a stationary population.

Dr. Garrett Hardin begins his paper on an economic note and develops his hypothesis of "the tragedy of the commons." Hardin recounts several examples of the unfortunate result of exploitation of the commons. In the development of the ecolate view, Hardin cites examples of the rich nations causing more harm than good as they seek to aid in the development of poor nations. He advocates the carrying capacity of the world nearer to its minimum rather than its maximum. Hardin raises many of the popular strategies for aiding the poor of the world and follows each with his "ecolate" question: "And then what?"

Social and natural scientists can explain the what and how of phenomena and perhaps the why of relationships. The why of decisions involves moral and ethical judgments. For this reason the response of the theologian-ethicist is annually invited to complete the discussion. Ian Barbour considers three criteria for resource ethics: justice, freedom, and sustainability. In doing so he provides evaluation of the works of Commoner and Hardin. He concludes with Biblical references as background for his final thoughts on social justice, long-term stewardship, human fulfillment and judgment and hope.

The topic, "Global Resources: Perspectives and Alternatives," and the selection of the participants in this XIVth Nobel Conference resulted largely from the efforts and imagination of Professor Robert Moline, Chairman of the Department of Geography at Gustavus Adolphus College. The editing task was greatly facilitated by the careful attention to detail by each of the authors.

GLOBAL RESOURCES

chapter 1
The Transition to Renewable Resources

Barry Commoner

This conference reflects a widely shared view that the global system in which we live is rapidly approaching a new, critical situation. For hundreds of years, societies that have differed greatly in their structure and organization have been based on the common goal of exploiting natural resources for the benefit of human beings. To varying degrees, this process has improved the conditions of human life. Now, however, the resources that have supported rising standards of living are rapidly becoming less available. As a result, developing countries cannot afford the resources essential to their development, industrialized countries face serious economic disruptions, and international competition for diminishing resources threatens world peace.

Although the problem derives from a basic physical fact—our present dependence on nonrenewable resources—its most crucial expression is political: that the exploitation of the planet's resources has been accompanied by the enormous inequities that have divided its inhabitants into the rich and the poor. In abstract terms, the solution to the physical problem is self-evident: a gradual replacement of nonrenewable resources with renewable ones. And, as we shall see, there are practical ways of achieving this transition. However, superimposed on this monumental problem is the overriding issue created by the huge economic inequities. This issue—poverty—is enormous in its scope and brutal in its impact. It dominates the physical problem because those nations that are rich—and, within them, those classes that are rich—have the power to determine the course of the transition to renewable resources. In such a transition there is the danger that the rich will use their power to maintain, and even improve, their own economic position, at the expense of poor people and poor nations.

1

Our task here is to find a way, despite the enormous complexities and intense political difficulties that encumber this problem, to understand it. It will not be easy. We will confront a number of tempting traps. Because the problem deals with profound questions about the human condition it is tempting to substitute philosophy for fact and submerge the discussion in a sea of aphorisms. Because the technical aspects of the problem seem to be alluring in their relative simplicity, it is tempting to reduce the more difficult social and political issues to biological ones—a process that is particularly dangerous because it can readily cloak a partisan political aim in seeming objectivity of science.

My concerns here are to outline the basic problems that arise from our present dependence on nonrenewable resources, to evaluate the possibility of achieving a transition to renewable resources, and finally to consider the relation of such a transition to the overriding problem of economic inequity. The basic facts about resource renewability that we need to consider can be set forth in the following series of propositions.

1. The availability of all other resources depends on the availability of energy.

The resources on which the production of goods and services depend can be divided into two main classes: matter and energy. Since matter cannot, of course, be destroyed (apart from the very limited conversion of matter by nuclear reactions to energy), it is essentially renewable. The amounts of the different elements—such as carbon, oxygen, nitrogen, and the various minerals—on the earth is constant. Despite their fundamental renewability, the accessibility of many mineral resources becomes reduced as they are used. The reason is that they undergo spontaneous chemical and physical changes; for example, iron oxidizes into rust and scatters. However, these changes can be reversed: iron oxides can be smelted into metallic iron; scattered deposits can be gathered. But this can be done only by expending energy. By expending sufficient energy, all mineral resources are fundamentally renewable. The practical example is the conservation of gold and other previous metals. Nearly all of such metals that have been mined over the course of human history are still available in useful form. Because they are highly valued, great care has been taken to avoid scattering them and, where necessary (as in the case of recovering silver from chemical processes such as photographic film), considerable energy is expended to recover them. There is no reason why iron or copper cannot be handled in the same way.

This means that, at least on theoretical grounds, material resources can be renewable in practice, provided energy is available. Thus the overall problem comes down to the renewability of energy.

2. Although energy is indestructible, its ability to do work is not.

From the laws of thermodynamics we know that energy is useful only insofar as it yields *work* and that work can be obtained only when energy flows from one place to another. In the process of yielding work, the ability of energy to yield work is always reduced. The First Law of Thermodynamics tells us energy is itself indestructible, but the Second Law tells us that its ability to do work—which is its only value—is nonrenewable.

3. Work (and therefore a work-generating source of energy) is essential to the production of all goods and services.

From the laws of thermodynamics we know that work must always be done if we wish something to happen that will not happen by itself. Since all the goods and services that meet our needs—houses, shoes, bread, automobiles, telephones and the messages they carry—do not happen on their own account, all of them require that work be done and therefore that energy be acquired and made to flow. Hence, everything that is produced and all economic value depends on the use of energy to generate work.

4. The availability of energy depends on its price, which in turn depends on the renewability of energy resources.

The basic reason for the energy crisis is that nearly all of the energy sources on which modern production systems rely (in the U.S., for 96% of that used)—oil, natural gas, coal, and uranium—are nonrenewable. Because these fuels were laid down only once during the earth's history, their deposits are limited in amount. Inevitably, as a nonrenewable energy source is depleted, the cost of producing it—and therefore its price—rises faster and faster as more is produced and increasingly less accessible deposits must be exploited. Thus, unlike the production of other goods, in which increased production is usually accompanied by a *decrease* in production costs, as the total amount of energy produced grows, the cost of production per unit *increases*. For example, in the U.S. a series of studies by the National Petroleum Council and the Federal Energy Administration shows clearly that production costs, and therefore prices (assuming a fixed rate of profit), of domestic oil will increase at a progressively faster rate with production. The price of domestic oil was expected to increase by $0.60 per barrel in the 5 years between 1970 and 1975, by $1.10/bbl in the next 5 years, and by $1.40/bbl in the 5 years after that. In the same way, according to a report of the Edison Electric Institute, as uranium production continues the price of uranium fuel is expected to rise by about $2 per pound between 1985 and 1990, by $5/lb between 1990 and 1995, and by $14/lb in the next 5 years. (These prices are given in constant 1970 dollars, to eliminate the effect of general inflation.)

The reason for the exponential rise in the cost of producing a unit amount of a nonrenewable resource such as oil is that there is a strong interaction between the act of finding and producing oil and the structure of the "crop" of accessible oil fields that remain to be found. When exploitation of the U.S. oil resource began in earnest at the turn of the century the largest, best-yielding, most accessible fields were the first ones found and brought into production. Production costs were only a few cents per barrel. But soon the big, easily exploited fields were exhausted and it became more costly to find and exploit the next best ones. At first, when the costs were reckoned in pennies per barrel, their gradual rise was hardly noticeable. But now, after nearly 100 years of exploitation, the cost per barrel is reckoned in dollars, and soon in tens of dollars, and the annual increase in cost is correspondingly large. Like the rate of growth of a 100-year-old bank deposit at compound interest, the rate of growth of oil production costs has become spectacularly rapid. Thus, the nonrenewability of a resource such as oil does not mean that it will become physically, totally depleted, but that it will become too costly to produce. We will exhaust not the oil, but our ability to pay for it.

5.   There is no substitute for energy in the production system.

Energy is a factor of production; like raw materials, labor, and machines, it is an essential ingredient in the production of goods and services. But when the cost of a particular factor of production rises, it is likely to be replaced by a less costly one. Can such a substitution halt the exponential rise in the price of energy? Resources have certainly been exhausted in the past. For example, in the U.S. the once-vast herds of buffalo were destroyed. In this case, the expected escalation in price certainly occurred; in the 10-year period from 1880 to 1890 in which the great buffalo herds were wiped out, the price of a buffalo robe increased about tenfold. Although as a species buffalo are of course an irreplaceable resource, if viewed as a source of food and clothing they are replaceable. The exponential rise in the cost of buffalo robes was made irrelevant simply by substituting less costly sources of food and apparel, and incidentally saving the species from extinction.

However, energy is different: there is no substitute for it. Whether provided by fuel-fed machines, by beasts of burden, or by people, work must be done in every production process, and work is generated *only* by the flow of energy. There is no way to avoid this thermodynamic imperative. The labor of people or animals can substitute for inanimate forms of energy, but only for certain limited production processes. Practically speaking, then, unless we are willing to forgo most of the advantages of modern industrial and agricultural production and transportation, we must use some nonliving sources of energy. Unlike the buffalo, energy cannot be replaced in the economy as its price escalates.

On these grounds there is no reason to foresee an end to the present exponential rise in the price of oil and the other nonrenewable fuels on which we depend. The conventional explanation for the rising price of oil is that, angered by U.S. and European support of Israel in the war with Egypt and Syria in October, the Organization of Petroleum Exporting Countries (OPEC), led by the Arab nations, cut back oil production, inducing a world-wide shortage that enabled the cartel to raise the price from $3.01/bbl in the summer of 1973 to $11.65/bbl on January 1, 1974. In fact, the real reason for the increased oil price originates in the United States, not in the Arab nations. In 1973, the Arab oil ministers were well aware that OPEC's largest customers, the U.S. oil companies, had announced in a report published a year earlier that the price of oil produced in the U.S., which had remained essentially constant for 25 years, would need to begin rising exponentially. In response, the OPEC oil ministers followed the normal business practice—that goods ought to be priced at what the market will bear—and raised their own price. The Arab-Israeli war only provided a convenient excuse. Thus, contrary to conventional wisdom, the escalating price of energy, which is the only real evidence of an energy crisis, originates not with the greed and hostility of Arab shieks —however real that might be—but with the inevitable economic outcome of the depletion of oil in the United States (abetted, to be sure, by the oil companies' deliberate increase in their targeted rate of profit).

6.   The rising price of energy is a powerful inflationary force.

Because energy is used in producing all goods and services, when its price rises the cost of everything else is driven upward. Before 1973 U.S. commodity prices had been inflating at a modest rate of about 2% a year; after 1973 they took off, going into double-digit figures in 1974, and since then running at more than 10% a year. Consumer prices have not been far behind. Thus, the rising price of energy has become a driving force behind the rapid rate of inflation.

7.   Energy-driven inflation places a particularly heavy burden on the poor.

Inflation is a notorious evil; it reduces purchasing power, lowers the demand for goods, depresses production, and so leads to unemployment. The prices of goods that are particularly dependent on energy are hit hardest by the rising price of energy. These energy-intensive goods include housing (which depends on the cost of fuel and electricity), clothing (most of which is now made from petroleum-based synthetic fabrics), and food (which now heavily depends on fertilizers and pesticides, chemicals made out of petroleum and natural gas). This puts a particularly heavy burden on poor families, which use a much larger part of their budgets to buy such necessary, energy-intensive items, as compared with wealthier families. According to an analysis of 1976 consumer expenditures by the Exploratory Project for Economic Alternatives, the poorest 10% of U.S. households (with annual incomes of less than $3000) spent nearly 30% of their income on energy-intensive purchases; middle-income families spent 7.4% of their budget on such purchases; and the wealthiest 10% of U.S. families spent only 4.2% of their income in that way.

8. The rising price of energy tends to hamper new industrial investments.

Since 1973 the price of energy has been rising at a rate unprecedented in the history of the country. In the 10 years before 1973 the energy price index increased at about 3.7% per year; in the years from 1973 to 1976 it has been increasing at the rate of 25% per year. The high *rate of increase* in energy costs inhibits new capital investment. Between 1950 and 1970, when energy prices were stable, the entrepreneur could count on an accurate forecast of future energy prices when predicting the operating costs of a new enterprise. With energy prices now rising so rapidly future prices are very uncertain, and the risk that a new investment will fail is increased. A number of business commentators have pointed to such uncertainties as a major cause of the present slow rate of investment—which means that plants are not built, and job opportunities are lost.

9. The present energy system wastes capital.

The availability of capital, and the willingness of investors to risk it in new productive enterprises, is essential to the economy's health. There is a close connection between the flow of energy and capital. Present forms of energy production are extraordinarily capital intensive—that is, relative to the economic value of its output, energy production demands much more capital than other productive enterprises. As a result the energy industry is particularly vulnerable whenever it becomes difficult to raise investment capital. This often leads to the abandonment or delay of energy projects that are especially capital intensive, such as nuclear power plants and synthetic oil and shale oil projects.

Various ways of producing energy differ considerably in their capital productivity—that is, in the yield per dollar of capital invested. The most recent analysis of this problem by the American Gas Association shows, for example, that to deliver one quad of energy per year to residential/commercial users, an electric power plant system would require an investment that is more than twice that required for systems based on natural gas. For industrial use there is a 3-to-1 disparity between the capital required by the two types of energy systems. The production of coal is considerably more capital intensive than the production of oil or natural gas. The production of synthetic oil from coal, or shale oil, is also particularly capital intensive. The present emphasis on electric power, especially from nuclear plants, and on the production of coal and synthetic fuels is wasteful of investment capital.

From these considerations it can be seen that, although the energy crisis originates in the nonrenewability of present energy sources, it is expressed not in the reduced production of these sources, but in their exponential rise in price. In this sense the energy crisis is fundamentally an *economic* crisis, which has a particularly important effect on the gap between the rich and the poor. In an industrialized country such as the U.S., the escalating price of energy places a growing burden on the poor and has become a chief reason for increasing difficulties with inflation and unemployment. In the world economy, the developing nations occupy an analogous position, relative to the rising price of energy, to poor people in the industrialized countries. In these nations the effort to develop industry, agriculture, and transportation is bound to be hampered when the cost of the energy—oil in particular—on which they depend escalates. The most disastrous effects of the sharply rising world price of energy that began with the 1973 embargo have been felt by poor people and poor countries.

It is ironic that this difficulty has been visited on the developing countries because of the way in which the U.S. has developed its own sources of energy. As already pointed out, in recent years, with the continued depletion of U.S. oil resources, production costs have risen to the point where their exponential increase has powerful economic effects. And with the rising cost of U.S. oil production, oil produced from much "younger" areas, such as the Mideast, although still relatively cheap to produce, could command a price that also rises exponentially. Thus, the depletion of the world's first major oil source—in the U.S.—has triggered a disastrous escalation of world energy prices.

The resulting economic difficulties can only be resolved by a transition from the present dependence on nonrenewable energy sources to use of renewable sources whose cost will be stable with time. Such a transition must begin at once if we are to avoid the catastrophic economic effects of further escalation in energy prices. Hence the choice must be made, now, between the two possible existing forms of renewable energy: nuclear power supported by a breeder reactor system (which would extend the availability of nuclear fuel to perhaps 1500–2000 years) and solar energy.

The nuclear breeder alternative would have many highly undesirable consequences: imposition of enormously risky and as yet unmanageable problems of dealing with radioactive wastes; a growing danger of proliferation of nuclear weapons; the consequent military control of power installations; the huge amounts of capital required; the resultant isolation of energy sources from control of the users of energy; and the danger of economic and political dominance of society by whatever agency controls these sources.

In contrast, the solar alternative is environmentally benign and in no way endangers peace. Solar energy is universally distributed and is especially available in developing countries, and acquisition of solar energy usually involves no economy of scale, so that it is equally efficient in whatever size is most appropriate to the task—large units of capital are therefore not essential.

The common response to the suggestion that the immediate introduction of solar energy is the solution to the energy crisis is that this is something for the distant future. But this is a tragically false perception. The fact is that for most methods of using solar energy the technology is already available and can be introduced at once for a variety of uses at economically competitive costs. It is useful here to summarize the basic propositions that govern the realistic introduction of solar energy.

1. The cost of producing solar energy will not escalate, but will remain stable as production expands.

Unlike oil, natural gas, coal, or uranium, solar energy is renewable; it will never run out (or at least not in the next few billion years). Because solar energy is renewable it is not subject to diminishing returns, which means that its price, instead of escalating like the price of present energy sources, will be stable and will even fall as the cost of devices continues to decline. By stabilizing the price of energy, solar energy reduces the threat of inflation and eases the task of planning investments in new productive enterprises, thus relieving two of today's worst economic problems—inflation and unemployment.

2. Solar energy is available everywhere, but the most accessible forms vary from place to place.

The use of solar energy does not depend on any single technique. There are different sources of solar energy, some forms more available in one place and other forms in other places. Everywhere that the sun shines solar energy can be trapped in collectors and used for space heat and hot water. Of course, the amount of sunshine varies from place to place, but not as much as most people think. The sunniest place in the United States, the Southwest, gets only twice as much sunshine as the least sunny place, the Northwest. In some places the most available form of solar energy may be wind (the wind blows because the sun heats the air on the earth's surface unevenly). In agricultural areas solar energy will be available in the form of organic matter (which is produced by plants, through photosynthesis, from sunshine): manure, plant residues, or crops grown to be converted into methane (the fuel of natural gas) or alcohol. In forest areas waste wood, or even wood growth for the purpose, can be converted into heat either directly or by being made into methane. And wherever the sun shines, photovoltaic cells can be used to convert solar energy directly into electricity.

3.   The necessary solar technologies are immediately available.
Solar collectors are used all over the world, and about 30 years ago were common in Florida and California; small windmills used to dot the farm landscape; methane plants are in operation in hundreds of thousands of Indian and Chinese villages; alcohol produced from grain was used extensively, mixed with gasoline, to run cars and trucks during World War II; photovoltaic cells now power satellites and remote weather stations. Of course solar energy needs to be stored during the night or over cloudy periods. This can be done in batteries, in tanks of alcohol or methane, in silos full of grain, as standing timber, or for that matter in piles of manure. All these items exist.

4.   Some solar technologies are already economically competitive; all will eventually become competitive relative to nonrenewable energy sources.
As already pointed out, the cost of conventional nonrenewable fuel is now rising exponentially and will do so indefinitely. Since it is renewable, the cost of solar energy is fixed only by the cost of the equipment, which will fall in price as experience is gained. Place these two curves on the same time scale and inevitably they will sooner or later cross. Solar energy, which a few years ago was more expensive than the conventional alternatives, will inevitably equal them in price and then each year become cheaper relative to conventional energy.

Estimates of when and how solar energy systems become economically advantageous have now been made by the Solar Energy Task Force of the Federal Energy Administration (FEA; now part of the new Department of Energy). Some examples follow.

Solar heating   In most of the central part of the United States, if the government would provide low-cost loans, it would today pay a house-holder who uses electricity or oil for space heat and hot water to replace about half of it with a solar collector system. Even borrowing all the neces-sary funds at 8% interest, with a 15-year amortization period, would cut an average annual heating bill by 19%–20%.

Photovoltaic electricity   The FEA's report shows that the production of electricity from photovoltaic cell systems can compete with conven-tional power sources and shows exactly how that can be accomplished. The report shows that, beginning immediately for the more expensive installa-tions such as gasoline-driven field generators, within 2 years for road and parking lot lighting, and within 5 years for residential electricity in the Southwest, photovoltaic units can compete, economically, with conven-tional power. All that is required to achieve this remarkable accomplish-ment is for the federal government to invest about $0.5 billion in the pur-chase of photovoltaic cells. This would allow the government to order photovoltaic cells with a total capacity of about 150 million watts, an order that would allow the industry to expand its operations sufficiently to re-duce the price of the cells from the current price of $15/W (peak) to $2–$3/W in the first year, to $1/W in the second year, and to $0.50/W in the fifth year, achieving the competitive positions noted above and suc-cessfully invading the huge market for conventional electricity. At a price of $2–$3/W, photovoltaic units would be more economical than fuel-operated irrigation pumps or power stations in most developing regions of the world.

Methane and alcohol production from organic matter   Although methods of commercializing these sources of solar energy have not yet been worked out by the FEA's task force, current research has already be-gun to show how that can be done. Public works funds can be used effec-tively to rebuild urban garbage and sewage-sludge disposal systems so that they generate methane, which can help meet a city's energy demand. In certain farm operations, such as a dairy with 200 or more cows or a farm raising 5,000 or more chickens, it is already economical to replace current manure-disposal systems with methane generation, using it, for example, to produce electricity to drive farm machinery and heat to warm the barns. Several Midwestern states are actively developing alcohol production from grain as a partial substitute for gasoline in cars, trucks, and tractors.

5.   **The economic feasibility of solar energy depends on how it is inte-grated into conventional energy systems.**

A number of studies have shown that the economics of providing space heat can be optimized by integrating both the conventional and solar sources into a single system that is more flexible than either a purely solar or a purely conventional system. When sufficient sun is available relative to the concurrent outside temperature, the system is able to derive all the needed energy from the sun. On the other hand, when sunlight is scarce and/or the temperature is low the system can operate on conventional fuel. Because of this flexibility the complex system is able in the first situation to substitute cost-free sunlight for expensive fossil fuel and in the second one to substitute fossil fuel for a costly expansion of the solar system. The key to the economic feasibility of the combined system is that it is *integrated*—its solar and conventional parts are fitted together so as to use the system's dual capabilities when each of them gives the most favorable results. Naturally the relationship is not a static one: as the price of fossil fuel continues to rise exponentially it will become economically sound to give solar energy an increasingly larger role in the combined system.

Another example is provided by the FEA's photovoltaic commercialization plan. In this case the economic feasibility of introducing the solar technology was enhanced by integration at at least two different levels. In the first place the FEA's plan recognized the importance of integrating the initial production of photovoltaic cells into the overall economic structure of the market for electricity. In the past, it was customary to dismiss the possibility of introducing photovoltaic electricity by simply comparing the high cost of such power with the much lower cost of utility power. The FEA's approach was based on an understanding of the complex nature of the market for electricity, in particular that a small, but nevertheless significant, part of the market—that supplied by gasoline- or diesel-operated generator sets—uses electricity that costs much more (10 to 50 times) than average utility power. The success of the FEA's commercialization scheme is based on the discovery that the immediate market for photovoltaic systems to displace conventional generators is so large that it would enable manufacturers to bring the price of the cells down to \$2–\$3/W in about one year. Moreover, once production facilities are expanded to meet this initial demand, the price continues to fall, enabling photovoltaic cells to compete in ever-larger markets. A second integrating feature of photovoltaic commercialization is described below.

6. The economic feasibility of solar energy also depends on integration with the energy-using process of production.

The high cost of storage is a major reason for the relatively large capital costs involved in solar technologies. This cost can be sharply reduced by incorporating the solar source into an energy-*using* system that itself has a built-in storage capability. Thus, if a photovoltaic system is used to provide power for an electric car, which must have a battery in order to operate (regardless of whether the electric source is conventional or solar), the high cost of storage normally needed in a photovoltaic system is eliminated. In the same way, an industry that found it useful to equip its workers with battery-operated hand tools (in place of tools that operate off the power line) in order to avoid the hazards of long electric cords would find photovoltaic electricity particularly economical. With two sets of storage batteries, one set could accumulate the photovoltaic power while the other set is used in the plant. Again, integration, this time between energy source and energy-using task, is the secret to successful economic introduction of solar energy.

These considerations show that to be economically successful a solar technology should not be considered as an isolated piece of equipment. It is a mistake to develop a solar technology autonomously and then judge it, with respect to its economic efficiency, against some other equally isolated conventional technology. Rather, the foregoing examples show that commercially successful solar energy can be introduced only if it is regarded as an integral part of an overall system of production. The advantages and disadvantages of the solar technology must be carefully matched to the capabilities and difficulties inherent in the system as a whole. Solar energy can best be introduced when it improves the economic efficiency of *the production system as a whole*.

7. The present energy system must be modified to facilitate the solar transition.

Although solar energy cannot be effectively introduced unless it is integrated into the energy and productive systems as a whole, the present systems are so faulty that fitting a new solar technology into them is often likely to fail for that very reason. In other words, we are confronted here by a "bootstrap" problem. The solar transition requires a transformation of *both* the energy system as a whole and of its constituent technologies.

This problem can be solved by recognizing first, that the purpose of introducing solar energy is not to satisfy some cultural longing but to accomplish an *economic* purpose. Second, there are nonsolar steps that can be taken to achieve this same purpose that will so alter the overall structure of the energy system as to facilitate the introduction of solar energy. This is the strategic basis for a realistic solar transition. An essential feature of a solar transition is the *replacement of existing energy-using* devices that are incompatible with a solar source with comparable devices that can be operated on either a conventional or solar energy source. An oil- or coal-burning heating system is a good example of solar incompatibility, since the production from a solar source of an equivalent fuel capable of being used in such a system is likely to be difficult. In contrast, a heating system that burns natural gas can operate either on that fuel or on a solar fuel—methane produced from organic wastes or crops. Such a system would be an essential bridge between the conventional energy system and its solar replacement. In the same way decentralized operation and high thermodynamic efficiency will also aid the development of the solar system.

8. Cogeneration of heat and electricity from natural gas plays a crucial role in the solar transition.

In conventional electric power plants at least two-thirds of the energy available from the fuel is wasted—emitted into the environment as heat. Cogeneration, in which this wasted heat is put to use, is an ideal transitional process. The economic advantages of cogeneration have thus far been exploited for fairly large industrial and commercial installations. For example, a recent article describes a project, supported with initial funding from the Department of Energy, which is to build a cogenerator for downtown Trenton, New Jersey. It is expected to have an ultimate capacity of 37.5 megawatts. The unit is expected to have an overall efficiency of 63%, as compared with 30%– 35% for conventional power plants. It is expected to annually save $40,000 in energy production costs and 10,202 barrels of oil in comparison to a conventional power plant.

What is less well known is that cogeneration can also be used on a very small scale—down to a single house—if need be. The Fiat Company of Italy recently marketed a small cogenerator for a single-family home. It consists of a four-cylinder auto engine that drives an electric generator and supplies heat for space heating and hot water. It will run on gasoline, methane, natural gas, or alcohol. The unit can convert 66% of the energy input into heat and 26% into electricity; only 8% Is lost. (A conventional home furnace will convert 40% to 65% of input energy to space heat, with the remainder being lost.) For producing electricity alone, it is almost as efficient as a central electric generating station, not counting the available heat, which is of course lost in central power generation. The model marketed by Fiat costs about $200 per kW (electric) installed ($2,800 per unit), versus $500 to $1,500 per kW for central electric power plants.

The massive installation of such units would not only save energy and utility costs; it would also create jobs in the auto industry and in maintenance and repair work, and would decentralize energy production and establish a base for efficiently introducing solar energy. Ideally, the size of the cogenerator should be matched, economically, to the size of the task. Thus, in rebuilding an urban neighborhood, it might pay to include a small cogenerator that would provide all the rehabilitated buildings with space heat, air conditioning, and electric power—probably selling some electricity to the utility as well. In this way increased electric capacity would be automatically linked to new demand, the costly overcapacity inherent in the present centralized systems avoided, and the introduction of solar energy facilitated. Here is an answer not only to rising utility bills, but also to the feeling of helplessness that tends to overwhelm consumers when they confront the giant utilities. This too is one of the advantages of a solar transition.

Such a cogeneration system effectively facilitates the transition to solar energy. Three different sources of solar energy can be readily introduced with relatively small changes in the system itself. Solar collectors can be readily introduced by feeding the heat that they collect into the system's existing heat storage and transfer system. At the same time, panels of photovoltaic cells can be installed to provide a good part of the needed electricity. Moreover, methane from a solar source can be substituted for at least part of the natural gas that fuels the cogenerator. In the U.S., based on expected availability of biomass methane, this could reduce the amount of fossil fuel now used to supply the residential/commercial sector by 87%.

It would pay to replace existing oil- and natural gas-fired heating systems with units of this type. It would benefit the immediate consumer economically; it would result in enormous savings of fossil fuel; it would achieve the kind of decentralization essential for the effective operation of a solar system. A comparison with nuclear power is informative. In 1987 a 1000-MW nuclear power plant will probably cost $1 billion. The same electric capacity could be achieved by installing some 67,000 15-kW cogenerators at a total cost of $191 million. The nuclear power plant would produce electricity at a cost of $0.091/kWh, whereas the cogenerators would produce electricity at $0.023/kWh, and heat at the cost of the fuel used (all of the above sums are in 1975 dollars). Clearly it would pay to install cogeneration units in place of a nuclear power plant. Such a program would also begin to decentralize electricity production and so pave the way for localized photovoltaic systems.

Fundamental to such schemes is the crucial importance of natural gas. Because cogenerators must be close enough to residential and commercial consumers to efficiently supply them with heat, cogenerators must be compatible with an urban environment. Only a cogenerator fueled by natural gas, which releases only carbon dioxide and water when it is burned, can meet this requirement. Natural gas is also the only fossil fuel that can be replaced by a solar fuel—methane generated from organic matter—with no change in the energy-using equipment. It therefore facilitates the gradual introduction of solar energy without excessive disruptions and costs. (It is worth noting that this process is already under way in Chicago, where the gas utility is buying methane produced from manure at a cattle feedlot in Oklahoma at $1.97 per 1000 cubic feet. The solar methane is being pumped into the Texas-Chicago natural gas pipeline and delivered to Chicago consumers as a very small proportion of the gas that they are now burning in their furnaces and kitchen stoves.) For these reasons natural gas is the essential "bridging fuel" in the solar transition.

9.   There are sufficient resources of fossil fuel in the U.S. to sustain a gradual transition to solar energy.

Taking the foregoing propositions into account, it is evident that the U.S. could in time accomplish a gradual transition from our present nearly total dependence on nonrenewable fuels to a nearly total use of solar energy. Recent analyses show that the process could probably be largely completed over a 50-year period. But this can be accomplished only if the available supplies of conventional fuels, and natural gas in particular, are sufficient to sustain this transition.

In such a transition the present use of coal, oil, and nuclear power could be gradually reduced to zero over the 50-year period, and oil imports could be eliminated in 20 years. But the present annual consumption of natural gas (about 20 trillion cubic feet) would need to be increased to about 35 trillion cubic feet over the first 25 years. It could then be reduced, over the following 25 years, to about 5 trillion cubic feet. It is important to note that no national system could be *completely* solar until it had enough excess capacity to allow for storage. Like all processes that depend on sunlight (such as farming), the output of a national solar system would depend on the weather. We could not afford to run out of energy in a bad year, so a standby energy source is essential. Again, natural gas is the leading candidate since it could be quickly produced from capped-off wells, distributed in the pipelines used for solar methane, and burned in the equipment that uses the latter with no change.

These ideas seem strange when viewed against the common conception—so dramatically expounded by President Carter when he introduced the National Energy Plan last year—that we are "running out" of oil and natural gas. Of course we are "running out" of these fuels; this has been true ever since the first barrel of domestic oil was taken out of the ground in 1859. The relevant question is how much remains to be produced, and at what price. In the context of the above considerations the crucial question is whether there are remaining supplies sufficient to sustain the transition to solar energy.

This is a complex and often confusing area, in which it is easy to get the wrong answer by the simple expedient of asking the wrong question. For our purposes the relevant question is not how long the *known,* already located resources of fuel will last, but rather how long the much larger *unknown* resources still to be located will last. Although answers to this last question are necessarily uncertain, the most recent data available from the U.S. Geological Survey indicate that the potential resources of domestic oil in the U.S. could supply the nation's needs (at the present rate of consumption) for about 70 years. Similarly, a recent report from the Petroleum Industry Resource Foundation indicates that the world supply of oil is probably enough to meet present world demand for about 80 years. Thus oil supplies are quite sufficient to sustain a 50-year transition to solar energy, during which the present rate of oil consumption would be gradually reduced to zero.

For the reasons already cited, the most crucial question is whether the potential supply of natural gas is sufficient to serve as the "bridging fuel" in a solar transition. The potential supply in the U.S. was evaluated by industry experts at a recent seminar conducted at the Aspen Institute. Taking into account existing conventional resources and natural gas available from newly developed deep sources, it was estimated that annual production would rise from the present level of 20 trillion cubic feet to 35 trillion cubic feet by the year 2000. The total size of the resource is estimated at 1500–2000 trillion cubic feet from conventional sources and 10,000 trillion cubic feet from the new, deeper sources. The newer gas can be produced at a price of about $5/thousand cubic feet—a price that conventional gas is expected to reach within 10 years. Clearly there is enough of this crucial fuel available to support a 50-year solar transition in which annual consumption would rise to 35 trillion cubic feet in the first 25 years and then fall to 5 trillion cubic feet in the next 25 years. A great deal of natural gas would then remain to serve as a standby fuel for many years or until production of solar methane is large enough to produce a surplus for storage.

The foregoing consideration describes, at least in part, some of the factual background to the vexatious problems that are being generated by the decreasing accessibility of the nonrenewable resources on which we depend. Although these observations are largely based on the U.S. situation, they are relevant to the world situation as well. The chief reason is that the real impact of the energy crisis—the escalating cost of oil and other fuels—although it affects the world, has its origin in the status of the U.S. oil resources. Once the U.S. remedies its present dependence on oil, there will be no reason why the world price of oil should be determined by the cost of producing the oldest, most heavily exploited, and therefore most expensive resource—U.S. domestic oil. Thus, as the U.S. undertakes the solar transition the world price of oil could be governed, more reasonably, by the lower costs of producing it from the much newer fields in the Mideast and elsewhere. The escalating world price of oil and other fuels could then be checked, facilitating the solar transition everywhere in the world.

It should be recalled, also, that the sun shines everywhere on the earth and that developing countries, which are largely in the tropics, are particularly well blessed with this renewable resource. All of the sensible forms of solar energy—solar collectors, windmills, fuels from organic matter, and even photovoltaic cells—can be applied in developing countries almost as readily as they can in industrial ones. All of these forms can be efficiently applied at whatever scale matches the need. No huge capital investments, which are not readily available to developing countries, are needed. There are, of course, *unreasonable* forms of solar applications that imitate the huge, centralized design of present conventional sources, such as centralized solar electric power stations, or even the proposed huge (and grossly unrealistic) solar satellite. These forms are unreasonable because they ignore one of the crucial differences between conventional and solar energy sources. The former have a large economy of scale, so that the efficiency of a large centralized plant can support the extra cost of the necessary transmission network. But solar installations have no economy of scale (that is, since solar energy is horizontally distributed, large energy-catching units are achieved by adding together numerous smaller ones, so that efficiency is independent of overall size) and do not produce savings that can support the network needed in connection with centralized plants.

Thus, applied sensibly, solar energy can be efficiently used on whatever scale is appropriate—from a solar water heater in a single dwelling, to a solar-powered irrigation pump in the villages of developing countries, to a neighborhood power plant in an industrialized city.

Finally we must return to the overriding economic, social, and political issue of poverty. How does this relate to the foregoing considerations? First, we must take note of the melancholy fact that some advocates of solar energy—among them President Carter—believe that the only way to encourage the introduction of solar energy is to raise the price of conventional energy even faster than it is increasing at present. The reasoning is that the sooner the cost of conventional energy overtakes the high cost of a solar installation, the more people will be encouraged to make the solar investment. The trouble is that this inducement will work only with those people who possess the capital needed to meet the high initial cost of a solar installation (which is about $15,000 to heat a typical one-family home)—that is, the rich. Meanwhile, the poor, who cannot afford to switch to solar, would be burdened by an unnecessary increase in the already high cost of conventional energy. This scheme is Robin Hood in reverse; it would take from the poor and give to the rich. It would force the poor people in both a single country such as the United States and in the poor countries of the world to bear the economic burden of a solar transition.

The answer, I believe, lies in social action that would govern the production and pricing of energy in the interest of carrying out the solar transition in an equitable manner. Here I reflect a political point of view that will not be shared by every participant in this symposium. I believe that the great global transformation that must end our present, catastrophic dependence on nonrenewable resources—the solar transition—ought to be designed not only to achieve this purpose, but also to end poverty, within nations and among them. There is a contrary view, which will be voiced here, that poverty in the overpopulated developing countries ought to be treated with "benign neglect" (to cite one of the least harsh proposals) on the grounds that the world's resources cannot support its growing population, which must be reduced by attrition among those with the least sufficient access to resources—the poor, developing nations.

However, it is simply not true that the poverty of developing nations means that the earth has insufficient resources to support its present population. It is a fact, for example, that the present annual world production of food is enough to provide an adequate diet for 8 billion people—more than twice the world population. Some people in the world are poor and suffer from the hunger, disease, and despair that is the price of poverty— because other people are rich.

Some people believe that the root cause of the world's problems with depleting resources is the rising population. But this is a simplistic notion that attempts to reduce world politics to the more tractable form of biology. We know from a number of factual analyses of this problem that the dynamics of *human* populations (as distinct from animal populations) is governed by forces that are peculiar to people—in particular, that people desire (and produce) fewer children when living standards are high enough to ensure that their children will live long enough, and that society will be sufficiently wealthy, to provide them with a secure old age. The world has enough wealth to support its entire population at a level that appears to convince most people that they need not have excessive numbers of children. The trouble is that the world's wealth is *not* evenly distributed, but disproportionately divided among moderately well-off and rich countries on the one hand and a much larger number of people and countries that are very poor. The poor countries have high birthrates because they are extremely poor, and they are extremely poor because other countries are extremely rich. The answer, I believe, is not to reduce the number of poor people, so that their needs will no longer threaten the security of the rich, but to redistribute the world's resources, so that the poor have the incentive, and the means, of improving their own lives.

This, I believe, ought to be the great purpose of transforming the economy of the world from its present, catastrophic dependence on nonrenewable resources to the balance and stability that is endowed by the endlessly renewable global resource—the sun.

chapter 2
Benevolent Yokes in Different Worlds

Latitia Obeng

There is a world—an only world
Unique among all worlds—
It floats in kindly layers of airs
that both protect and feed life.
Its watery blues and grassy greens
Its sandy golds and earthy browns
In rising suns and waning moons
with whistling winds and booming seas
and whispering trees and thundering storms
reflect its treasures—boundless beauties and gifts—
a kaleidoscope of sound and sight!

I wonder how many people consciously appreciate that the air that is so vital for our living is all provided ready for us to breathe. We do not produce a sniff of it, and we take it for granted.

Nor do we, for extensive use, make even a drop of the water that is so indispensable for our physiology. Of course, we do desalinate sea water by laborious means and at great expense, and we succeed in harvesting dew and persuading clouds to drop rain. But the water is already there, in roaring seas, in sparkling dew, in dark tempestuous clouds, in rolling rivers, in expansive lakes, and even underground—ready for our taking.

Neither did we make even a tiny one of the many plants and animals that provide us with our food. It is true that we have developed new strains and improved hybrid vigor, but the parent plants and animals are part of the resources of this planet—provided and ready for our use as food in our many strange ways—as sour rhubarb, leafy artichokes, flying termites, chocolate-covered ants, rattlesnake steak, bamboo shoots, cole slaw, and even sea slugs!

The air, the water, and the food are absolutely essential and indispensable for our kind of physiology. These, as well as the raw materials that we need for clothing and shelter and good health, all basic needs for our peculiar human body, as well as all the other imagined (but often quite unnecessary) and extravagant needs, are available, or can be made available, and are in abundance from our natural resources. Gifts from a benevolent planet!

We are rather lucky that these resources are available, and more than lucky that they suit our human needs. Over the centuries, through our various ancestries, we have adjusted to using them. Human life as we know it now functions because these natural resources are available and also because we are physiologically tuned to their use. We are adjusted to using oxygen (which is kept abundant by a planetary system) and not sulfur dioxide or helium or some other not-so-abundant gas; we function on water (which is kept abundant, in spite of man, by a planetary hydrological system) and not on mined oil or plant nectar or some other not-so-easily-available liquid substance. Maintenance of human life is part of an unbreakable and closely linked chain formed by our resources, their rational management and protection, their continued viability, and the sustenance of sound environmental quality. It is our privilege to be responsible for the proper function of the chain that in turn assures our continued survival.

But are we really lucky that we depend so heavily on and can use these resources? Is this an unqualified act of benevolence from our planet? Do we have these gifts without any conditions? It would seem so from the viewpoint of our planet, the benefactor. For we now have, and have always had, the physical lands of the earth to grow our food—its soils and rocks have been around for ages and have not disappeared with time. The air still circulates in spite of our polluting activities; the waters have not completely evaporated or disappeared over the millions of years that they have been around. These will perhaps continue to be part of the planet forever, on a permanent basis, as gifts from our planet.

If there should be any conditions associated with these gifts of benevolence, they need to be set by ourselves out of gratitude for them and also in recognition of the responsibility placed on us for effective stewardship of the gifts that have been so benevolently bestowed upon us. It is a responsibility that we cannot and must not shun. Our continued living depends on the care and attention that we give to these our life-sustaining gifts of resources, renewable and nonrenewable—a kindly and indispensable bother of gifts—a yoke to which the satisfactory physiological functioning of the human body is unavoidably anchored. But it seems a yoke because we do not readily accept the responsibility that goes with the gifts. It ceases to be a bother when we all accept a collective responsibility for this stewardship.

The objective of this XIVth Annual Nobel Conference is to focus attention on our global resources—not so as to dwell on past mismanagement and waste, but so as to consider alternatives for better management of the planetary stores on genuinely environmentally sound lines and for the benefit of man and his planet.

At present, we do not really lack resources. We do not lack technologies either; we have so far used our technologies and resources to improve life quality. Now more than at any other time, more people are assured of better living, but there are many more who have not benefited adequately. We have not also always managed our resources effectively to assure their continued viability. As I see it, we have one alternative for the future, and it is for a dual purpose. Our new vision should be not merely toward better resource stewardship and effective management, but also to assure an equitable use of the resources for the benefit and good of all mankind.

I see this as the only alternative open to us, although in the present world situation I believe I deserve to be considered naive or even stupid for advocating such an alternative. Whoever considers me so may be justified, and for good reason. For decades now, mostly out of greed but also out of fear and a sense of insecurity, we peoples of the world have identified, established, and accepted various worlds—developed, developing, underdeveloped/least-developed; industrialized, nonindustrialized; First, Second, Third and Fourth "worlds." And we unconsciously look on them as permanent institutions.

Synonymous with these are levels of development and the availability of resources and amenities; there are those who have more than an adequate share of human needs on one hand and, on the other, those who lack the minimum of the basic needs of water, food, clothing, shelter, and good health. Even now the World Bank estimates that 800 million people in the Third World are living in absolute poverty.

If we are looking for a new vision, I cannot see a more logical or pressing course to follow than to stop making excuses and to use efficiently our technologies and resources to ensure that all people are adequately supplied at least with basic needs. Correcting this situation is a fundamental requirement to which our attention should be drawn and riveted as a basis for the alternative that we are now seeking.

I like to believe that we have not come here to listen to theoretical platitudes about what to do, but to genuinely evaluate precedents and explore alternatives. It is therefore not my intention to recite data or even discuss technical aspects of better resource management. We already know them. We also know how to improve on present practices that we consider unsatisfactory. The world is now quite sensitized to the need to preserve our natural resources and the human environment. I believe that what we now need is the discipline and willpower to do the things that we know should be done the best way that we know how, and to do them not for the benefit of the few, but for all.

I wish to concentrate on identifying and discussing some of the simple but fundamental problems that we need to redress if indeed we sincerely wish a new vision. I am convinced that I am not alone in seeing the way forward for us as a firm commitment to resource stewardship as I have interpreted it. Failing this, we would merely be paying lip service to the improvement of a world situation that so obviously needs genuine attention, and we would be wasting our time.

The equity of using our planetary resources for the benefit of all the planet's citizens should not be based on some ill-defined factors such as "cultural sensitivities" or "technological appropriateness"—whether they relate to life in either the Fourth, Third, Second or First "world." Cultural sensitivites are, really, chosen attitudes and forms of behavior whose evolution is conditioned by the availability of resources for development and survival.

It may be wrong, for instance, to interpret it as cultural preference if a people are even now dependent on meagre rations of firewood for energy while they have always sat on top of huge deposits of coal. If they had access to the coal, they could have evolved a way of using it, and perhaps developed a different cultural pattern. Similarly, those who have access to a coal-based energy source and the potentials that go with it have developed along a different cultural line. The two groups have followed divergent lines by choice, but a choice conditioned by available and accessible resources. By the same token, it also does not mean that the normal rural Asians or Latin Americans or Africans in developing countries prefer paraffin lights or candles or firewood torches to electric lights. They would also like to use electricity, once they have overcome any prejudices, not because the former kind of lighting is not sophisticated but simply because the latter is more convenient and more effective for lighting.

Although differences in regional facilities may be interpreted as preferences in the matter of the use of global resources, we need to make the basis for effective use quite clear, and not cloud the issues with indeterminate factors. We now have to discuss attitudes, principles, and activities that militate against effective use of our resources for the benefit of all mankind.

Long before us, in other civilizations and cultures on this planet, others looked on the earth's resources as gifts for which they had the responsibility as custodians. In my part of the world, for instance, in the

Ashanti kingdom—a fairly large ethnic group that had established a rich culture long before outsiders arrived in the area—the earth was very much revered. It was called "Asase Yaa," which meant Mother Earth Yaa—Yaa being the name of any woman born on a Thursday. Thursday was therefore made sacred to the Mother Earth, which was also a deity. The land was accepted as sufficiently important that prayers were offered to it at the start of the tilling of the land. The point that is even more relevant to this subject is that even Asase Yaa did not own the land; it was owned by others more powerful and long dead. The people in succeeding generations therefore merely held the land as tenants and in trust, on behalf of the dead and for those of the future, and traditional observances were instituted to promote responsible stewardship. Similar traditions were associated with lakes and lagoons on which, to this day, fishing is banned for specified periods of time. It is obvious that this practice also, whatever the traditional explanation, favored regulated harvesting of fish. Similar practices and observances are also found among other peoples in Africa and among the American Indians, in Asia, in the Pacific, in Papua, New Guinea, and in the parts of the world where people still live close to nature. Such beliefs in the importance of our planet and its resources and the reverence due to it in the course of its use were common in many ancient religions and, in their way, contributed to the practice of sound management of natural resources and conservation.

It would seem that something went wrong somewhere along the line. We have made enormous and really great advances in a comparatively short period of planetary time that have made life better for us than at any time on this planet. We still have problems, yes—diseases, famines, wars—but we have achieved a high level of life even though globally, it sometimes really shows only in brackets and pockets. In previous times there was no way of saving starving people; they died. We were helpless in epidemics; people died. We are still powerless against floods, typhoons, tidal waves, hurricanes, and earthquakes, but we can help affected nations. We can transplant hearts and kidneys, we can produce test-tube babies, and soon freezing the living to preserve them for the future will not be fiction! However, it would seem that we reckoned without much attention to the high productive powers of man.

Then, suddenly, we realized that we had more mouths to feed, and for many more years than previously, and that requirements had multiplied. Animal stocks, already capable of multiple births, had also increased and there was demand for more animal feed and grazing land. More land was needed for more food; where agricultural practices had been inadequate, the fertility of the land was threatened; forests that had stood long before us were being hacked down; catchment areas were disturbed; there was erosion, and flooding. And, with all these headaches, there were more people to feed, clothe, and house; more human and industrial wastes; more and more pollution of inland surface and groundwaters, the seas and the oceans, and the air—until mercifully the countries of the world pleaded STOP! We cannot go on like this, the resources are becoming depleted; their quality has been greatly degraded; we cannot maintain the high level of life that we have reached if we do not stop increasing our numbers and destroying our land, water, and air.

Within a decade, through the organization of the United Nations, the countries of the world have conferred about the environment, population, food, water, housing, desertification—current situations have been examined, alternatives considered, and resolutions and action plans made. It is well agreed that the poorest countries should receive attention. But how do we spread the good life standard to all inhabitants who should have it as a right with the present uneven spatial distribution of resources and the uneven demands put on them? How do we produce more food from the land with the threats that our present agricultural practices pose? How do we use the land when there are water shortages? And where water is available, how do we avoid waterlogging and salinization? How can we afford the fertilizers and pesticides and all the chemicals and the machinery needed for food planting, harvesting, processing, and distribution? How do we handle these with receding energy resources?

Permit me to repeat, I believe that what we now need is not so much resources but a different approach based on changed attitudes and principles for rational use and with the objective of providing for all. I shall illustrate by looking at aspects of the development and management of one of our vital resources, water.

But before then, let me draw attention to a matter that unless corrected, may remain a psychological barrier to change, whatever the alternative innovations that we may introduce. I stress the artificial compartmentalization of the world community into the First, Second, Third, and Fourth "worlds." At the upper end of the hierarchy is the First "world," most developed and richest; at the bottom end, the least developed and the poorest Fourth "world." I am referring to these artificial "worlds" because I believe that, psychologically, the hierarchical structure of these "worlds" on this planet is closely involved in the success of any global innovative activities that may be instituted toward an equitable use of resources for the good of all as a birthright.

If indeed this is the ultimate goal in which we are interested, then it becomes necessary that there be a clear understanding between the different "worlds." And, as I have indicated, sometimes by our attitudes one gets the impression that these "worlds" are seen as permanent institutions. If indeed we wish the earth's resources to be used for the good of all, then attitudes must change. For unless it is accepted that a good life is the birthright of all the rich shall continue to get richer and the poor, poorer. We have to decide whether more satisfactory development of life for all in the Third and Fourth "worlds" and for the poor of the First and Second "worlds" is a right of planetary citizenship, or charity. And this has to be settled before any substantial changes can be made by whatever alternatives we select.

Let me now examine this subject of alternatives further by focusing attention on water as one of our resources. It is old and abundant. We know that it covers two-thirds of the earth in the form of sea water (containing 35 parts per million of salts, and therefore unsuitable for human, and most plant, physiology. The proportion of it that is suitable and accessible for human use is only a fraction, less than 1%, but in quantity it is adequate for the use of a world population even larger than at present. The two main constraints that we already know are, first, it is unevenly distributed both as surface and groundwaters and as precipitation. There are world regions where rainful is a rare event, and others where floods are common. The problem attendant on this uneven distribution is an unsatisfactory water supply for human, domestic, industrial, and agricultural use in various parts of the world. It is estimated that two-thirds of the world's population do not have access to safe drinking water. It so happens that the greater part of the two-thirds live in the Third and Fourth "worlds."

The second constraint is that even where water may be available, its quality, without satisfactory treatment, quite often makes it unsafe for consumption. Rivers and lakes, especially those close to urban areas, suffer much from the industrial wastes that are dumped into them. This feature seems to be a problem in all four "worlds." The Thames, Seine, and Rhine are just recovering. In some developing countries, surface waters tend to get heavily contaminated, mainly by human domestic wastes, because of serious waste disposal problems. And in tropical regions of the Third "world" this makes surface waters transmitting sites and infecting sources for a number of water-dependent diseases.

There is also a further constraint. Rivers and streams are subjected to various forms of modification, and primarily to assure reliable water supply and also for fisheries, irrigation, hydropower generation, various forms of recreation, and navigation. In the process, balances are disturbed and there are ecological upsets with serious impact both on man and on his environment and its other resources.

In the use of water resources, it has been estimated that, in Pakistan alone, because of irrigation and bad drainage many hectares are destroyed through waterlogging and salinization. Hydroelectric power dams have been very much in vogue. In Africa, within a decade large dams—Kariba, Volta, Nasser, and Kainji—covered a total of 20,303 square kilometers, and others are under construction. There are also many millions of small impoundments in all four "worlds." In tropical areas, they also pose as problems, as do the large ones.

The impression must not be formed that these problems do not receive any attention. On the contrary, I believe it would be correct to say that, on the international scene, water supply activities, especially for the benefit of rural people, involve many organizations and large sums of money. In addition, there is an enormous effort being made by governments and numerous NGOs especially to assist with rural water supply. In spite of all this, the problem of rural water supply is being reduced only very slowly. Both the U.N. Water Conference and the Habitat Conference emphasized water problems and agreed on the importance of providing all people with safe drinking water. And I am convinced that we need to reexamine our present strategies and evaluate the reasons behind them. Specifically, it seems to me that we should revise our thoughts and attitudes to water supply in rural areas.

Let me deliberately provoke reactions on this personal observation. It seems to me that those who dedicate themselves to helping the rural poor with their domestic water supply somehow believe that the rural people are entitled only to a specific type of water supply system, different from what is provided for urban people. It is generally agreed that one of the very important reasons for improving rural domestic water supply is the impact that it can make on rural health. For this reason also, the water source has to be conveniently placed and adequate both in quantity and quality. So far, the best and most effective form of water supply that we know is water piped to homes. This is an accepted and almost automatic input for urban housing. And yet, somehow, when improvement to domestic supply in rural Third and Fourth World areas is designed, it turns out to be the provision of either a well or a borehole or a protected part of a spring, stream, or river, or at best a single or a few standpipes scattered around town.

I should like my concern to be seen in its right perspective. On a short term basis, such a strategy is reasonable. Unfortunately, if we examined the situation carefully, we would find that subconsciously such supply systems are considered adequate even on a long term basis—until the facilities break down. My concern is not with the "lack of sophistication" or "cultural unacceptability" or "inappropriateness of technologies," but with effectiveness and efficiency in solving a particular problem with a temporary solution that has been left too long, on a permanent basis.

Invariably long queues develop at village standpipes; the hand pump at the well breaks down; the windmill does not function. Then the busy villagers revert to unsatisfactory ponds and dry river beds to dig and scoop out dirty water, or to closer streams and dams that are transmission sites for various diseases or places where vectors of the diseases (mosquitoes, black-flies, tsetse flies) breed and are ready to bite and infect the unsuspecting people, thereby defeating a major purpose of the intended improvement of the domestic water supply system.

Because of unsatisfactory domestic water supply, rural women often carry their washing chores to the river. I get quite impatient with those First and Second "world" foreign experts who insist that it is part of the culture of rural African women to wash clothes away from home because it gives them occasion to a social event of riverside revelry with other rural women! The funny thing is that such experts cannot even communicate with the rural women to be told of a revelry that would obviously be in the company of mosquitoes and gnats and blackflies and tsetse flies, bilharzia snails, ants, and the occasional snake. Their linguistic worlds have nothing in common. And yet on such flimsy excuses more satisfactory washing facilities may be denied.

Do not miss my point. What bothers me is that, although we may all agree that wells and boreholes and protected springs (often with better water quality) are the realistic short term solutions, deep in the mind, most providers of resources automatically and perhaps unconsciously rule out piped water in favor of systems that they consider appropriate for rural areas, even on a long term basis!

Forgive me if I fuss over what may seem a trivial point. I have done so on purpose to illustrate one of the basic problems we should face if indeed this conference is seeking new and realistic alternatives for the future. I am realistic enough to know that not many will agree with me, for the usual reason given. Which is—piped water is expensive! I agree, and I shall again come back to this point. But now let us consider another aspect of rural water supply. There are other sources of water that may be satisfactor-ily tapped on an effective scale if only we would work on them. Rainwater and storm run-off water in some seasons are abundant where water is nor-mally scarce. There are even now many technologies that have been used by previous generations and civilizations to harvest rain and storm water for domestic use and there are technologies, including dew harvesting, that are in use now that can be improved on and promoted as additional

sources of water supply in appropriate areas. They are not sufficiently promoted. Perhaps they also seem expensive.

Let me also bring up another set of water problems for which change
in management strategy will be needed in terms of our future options. If
we take irrigation, the headaches are the loss of water through inefficiency
in the transportation of the water, excessive application of water, and inef-
ficient drainage systems. There are now irrigation technologies that are less
consumptive of water and that may be improved or adapted, but, the response is often given, they are expensive. Again, I shall pick up this point
later.

What about water resources development, and especially dams, in
tropical regions? They are very useful but they also cause ecological headaches. We know that they will cause headaches and we therefore have to
take precautions in the planning, construction, operation, and management of such dams. Control of the contact of people with such dams, the
discharge of industrial, agricultural, and domestic waste into them, fore-
stalling or at least keeping weed growth under control are important measures. We do know from experience how some of these problems have
arisen. We have reasonable strategies for controlling them—but they are
expensive and resources are never adequate to implement them.

I have given three instances of how some present water problems may
be tackled in developing countries. I see them as alternatives to some present strategies and practices and as new visions of what should be done in
the light of present and past experiences. I am advocating that, in improving rural water supply and water use in the Third and Fourth "worlds,"
strategies should not only be *appropriate* but, more importantly, they
should be *effective*.

I pick up now the point of effective water strategies being expensive. I
am afraid my reaction has always been, and always will be—*so what?* The
big cities of the world and also most old towns must also have been rural
areas at some time when they didn't have piped water, but rather perhaps
wells and boreholes and streams and windmills. They didn't stay with this
form of water supply, although piped water must have seemed expensive
in those days too. Perhaps people didn't even run the risk of river blind-
ness and bilharzia through daily trips to rivers. Why did they change?
They did so because safe, quality, convenient, adequate, effective water
supply is absolutely essential for good health and for much else besides,
and piped water is an effective supply system. Therefore, although expensive, resources were found on a long term basis for a reliable and safe water
supply.

Really, some of the excuses made to justify the inadequacy of rural water supply are ridiculous. I heard it said in a radio discussion that in rural developing countries people do not *need* as much water as urban people. I assure you that if she didn't have to spend half her day fetching a bucket of water, and it was there, on tap, the Third "world" rural woman would perhaps be as extravagantly irresponsible as her First and Second "world" urban counterpart, and more often than necessary soak herself in a full bath of local vitalizing herbs!

The argument of high expenses used in connection with concern over reducing the adverse environmental impact of irrigation, dams, and other water projects is equally flimsy. There has been no time in history that a country really needed resources and has not been able to beg, borrow, or bully others for it. It is a matter of determining priorities. In these instances, the improvements discussed are often not considered of priority importance.

Since we are looking for new vision, let us see the question of expense from another angle. We all know that it is never expensive to buy destructive arms and develop even more destructive ones and all four "worlds" indulge in this extravagance; it is never expensive to buy fast jets or build even faster ones; yet piped water for rural areas, on a long term basis, is considered expensive. I am assured that the resources used to obtain even one jet plane can provide piped water for some thousands of rural people. Globally, with such little sacrifice so much can be done. Even at our own individual level, if with others we collectively wasted less water brushing our teeth or changed the 5-gallon water flush system, the savings made would belie the excuse of expense given.

The alternative that we seek has to be rooted in a change of attitudes and hearts to establish a real sense of responsibility and a belief that all people deserve an equitable share of global resources; that provision of piped and effective water systems for the rural poor, for example, is not charity but a responsibility; that a reduction in overconsumption of the global resources by the privileged few, for example, is a responsibility and not a favor; that reasonableness is necessary for the use, conservation, and management of these many gifts from our benevolent planet.

> All creatures great and small have a right
>   to this planet.
> We have the responsibility to assure birds
>   their gentle glide in wholesome air; fish,
>   their graceful swim in safe waters;

the tiniest seed, the earth's goodness to
make it grow the mighty tree.
We have to assure burrows for rabbits, dens
for lions, lairs for foxes, and nests for birds;
we have to guarantee that worms can crawl in the
earth, the tortoise can shuffle on it, the snail
can slide its slimy path and the chameleon can
camouflage its slow journeys.

If, with the right attitudes, we can select and implement effective strategies and assure the right of all people to the resources of the planet, then surely we shall raise man higher by also providing effectively for these dumb creatures. If, in our frantic quest for material advance, we have left behind that little bit of moral quality needed for such responsibility, then let us look back, for the way forward now becomes the way back.

For decades the world acquiesced in injustices meted out by some world citizens to other world citizens. This has not stopped yet, not by any means; but we can cherish the hope that, through present world consciousness, in our lifetimes human rights will be permanently established for all peoples. Let it also be a real hope that in our lifetimes, additionally, the right to the basic human needs of adequate water, food, shelter, and good health, all products of our global resources, will indeed become a reality for those now deprived of this basic human right.

I trust that the concern for our planet and its resources and our future that has brought us here together will not fade with the end of this Conference but that, by our brief encounter here, we shall feel strengthened to urge others that we jointly accept our responsibilities to this our benevolent planet and its resources, and especially to our fellow men.

chapter 3
Projecting Economic Aspects of Alternative Futures

Tjalling C. Koopmans

It is a great pleasure and an exciting experience to be allowed and invited to come to this meeting. The conference, its theme, and the interest it arouses are signs of the times. Contemporary society is presented with new problems that have come to the fore in the last 10 to 15 years, although they could have been and to some extent were foreseen earlier. I note three traits that these new problems have in common. First, many of them are *interdisciplinary* in character in the sense that they involve a number of natural sciences—biological, physical, chemical, and engineering—and the social sciences, including economics—all because of the encompassing nature of these problems. Second, the problems also call for a *long time horizon*. I tend to think that the combination of these two traits of the new problems is the best thing that could have happened to economics. It has seemed to me that economics has been somewhat insular in communicating within the profession quite effectively in what, to people outside the profession, must look like some kind of jargon—like a secret society having its own language. This will become counterproductive, now that economists are increasingly called upon to sit on committees and to take their part in publications in which other sciences are represented and may even have the principal role. Third, these problems are also *international* in scope. In due course, solutions of these problems will depend on concerted action, and necessary steps toward such solutions will be international study, consultation, and possibly negotiation.

Many of the new problems involve present and future energy technologies, their possible impacts on the environment, and possible risks that

I am indebted to William C. Brainard and William D. Nordhaus for valuable comments on an earlier draft of this lecture.

may be associated with them. As an example, the use of fossil fuels, which has been a mainstay for our energy production and use, can continue for a long time still as far as coal is concerned, but time is measured with respect to oil and gas, although opinions differ as to how long supplies will last at reasonable cost. However, the combustion of all fossil fuels increases the concentration of carbon dioxide (CO_2) in the atmosphere. You will not notice its effect in breathing (it has no odor and is not a poison) but it may well have climatological effects.

The increase in the atmospheric concentration of CO_2 since the Industrial Revolution has been something like 10%. Now what are the effects of that? The climatologists don't know yet for sure. They are working hard on the problem, but they are as yet divided in their opinions. More observation and research will be needed before this is clarified. Meanwhile we shall want to follow their work and think through, supposing the effects were to be harmful, what policies would be needed. The principal concern has been that CO_2 does absorb the outgoing radiation from the earth as it is heated by the sun more than it absorbs the incoming radiation from the sun, so that a certain greenhouse effect is anticipated. These are reasons for concern about what that would do to the world's climate, to the level of the oceans if icecaps resting on land should melt, and to the conditions for agricultural production in various parts of the world. I bring this up as a problem that is unsolved, and that calls for intensive collaboration of several professions in many nations.

Other such problems are associated with the use of nuclear fission—a whole range of problems indeed, but let me mention just two. One is the problem of radioactive waste disposal, for which the United States is still searching for a safe disposal method and place. Another arises from the possibility that, as more advanced nuclear reactors, and in particular nuclear breeder reactors, are going to be put into use, serious risks of diversion or proliferation of weapons-grade nuclear materials may arise. I will come back to these problems later, mentioning them here only as other serious problems that have all three of the characteristics indicated above.

My principal concern in this exploration today is not with solutions. I have no recommendations to make. I am concerned with concepts and methods that may help in finding solutions. In particular I emphasize a device for interdisciplinary studies that I have had some involvement in, the calculation and comparison of long range projections into the future that are arrived at in collaboration between the disciplines. The natural scientist, biological, physical, or geological, contributes the basic assumptions about presently available or expected future technologies, and about availability of resources. The economist comes into the act by proposing or formulating the objective to be pursued and by contributing elements of the model that express how consumers and producers respond if prices and quantities are likely to change in the future. Examples of the quantities would be population growth, energy use, growth of gross national product, and any other variables that are pertinent to the particular problem. Prices would be either anticipated future *market prices* or, where the market does not reach, they could be computed as *shadow prices* of present and future goods and services. In what follows I illustrate the extension of the market prices by a system of shadow prices that refer to either good or bad things that are not or not yet evaluated in a market.

The projections, to come back to those once more, have the form of conditional statements. They assert: "If such and such, then so and so." Often the attention is drawn mostly to the "then so and so," but the "if such and such" is an indispensible part. No statement has been made unless the "ifs" have also been specified.

Both quantities and prices of economic goods and services are derived from, are implicit in, the technological possibilities and the chosen objective. I shall spend more time with the prices because these have given rise to recurring misunderstandings between natural scientists and economists. I shall build up and illustrate the concept of related quantities and prices in projections in four steps that I label A, B, C, and D. In each step I shall summarize the things I have to say in a list of propositions.

STEP A: MARKET VALUES AND SHADOW PRICES
OF PRESENT (CONTEMPORARY) GOODS AND SERVICES

I invite you to go back with me in the history of economic thought, to Adam Smith, and to the basically simple competitive model of the economy that he perceived and developed.

PROPOSITION A1. *A competitive market economy generates valuations of all competitively produced and traded goods and services, in the form of market prices. These values are relative, not absolute. They result from a balance between private cost of production and the willingness and ability to pay on the part of consumers.*

I note a few of the terms used here. Cost of production reflects existing technology and an assumption of cost-minimizing behavior of producing firms and individuals. The expression "willingness to pay" reflects the preferences of consumers, the term "ability to pay" reflects the distribution of income. I emphasize that this is a market model, and that Adam Smith did not in this model include goods and bads that are not transmitted through the market. These nonmarket effects, often called *externalities*, were introduced into economics by the British economist Alfred Pigou in 1920. They were reintroduced in 1968 among natural scientists by Dr. Garrett Hardin, who is here with us.

The following proposition sings a muted praise of Adam Smith's famous "invisible hand." The praise is muted because Smith limited himself to market effects and because the proposition does not deal with questions of distribution of income. The song is written in a contemporary idiom.

PROPOSITION A2. *Ignoring effects not transmitted through the market, the competitive equilibrium is efficient in the limited sense that, for given inputs of primary resources, no consumer can be made better off without another being made worse off.*

In less precise but more easily understood language: the price system guides the best use of the goods. Price reflects cost, and that is minimum cost, by the assumption already stated. Also, the consumer, who spends his income as best he can, is again guided by the price because, if a particular good is expensive, he will take away from his spending power for other goods if he buys that one good. Thus he is nudged by the price system into satisfying his own preferences to best effect.

Now about the effects that Adam Smith ignored. Not traded in the market are public goods such as parks, highways, police services, and any number of other goods and services arranged for by federal, state, or local governments, which are paid for out of tax revenue. There are also the bads, adverse externalities such as air and water pollution, airplane noise, and any other things that we have come to complain of, because their impacts grew as our satisfaction from regular goods grew—thus drawing more attention to what was lacking in the entire picture.

The externalities—that is, the nonmarket goods and bads—then are all desirable and undesirable effects of the production or consumption of goods on parties not involved in the transactions by which the goods change hands. Now, an approach of current environmental economics seeks to extend the price system so as to include also nonmarket goods and bads. The extended prices are called shadow prices because they are not directly observed in the market. Their computation is explained in the following two propositions.

PROPOSITION A3. *Through calculation the system of valuations can be supplemented by shadow prices of goods and bads that are not traded in markets. The public goods are valued at cost. The bads are valued by nega-*

tive numbers. These may reflect appropriate pollution penalties, or they may express incremental costs incurred in order to limit or correct environmental damage.

By way of example, if the upper bound on the quantity of a harmful substance that can be released through the exhaust pipe of an automobile is tightened, then an additional cost of clean-up of the exhaust gas must be incurred by the car manufacturer and by its owner. That cost can then be computed as the shadow price of that particular improvement of the environment.

PROPOSITION A4. *These calculations are meaningful only if the kinds and quantities of public goods and the penalties and constraints on adverse externalities are arrived at in a manner that reflects the desires of the voters or at least has their concurrence.*

In the same way as in the market operation of prices of consumer goods, to which consumers respond by their own purchases or abstentions, the shadow prices have a role. Through some process of political decision or toleration of allowed quantities of bads, these bads are evaluated by the social costs of bringing them down to the tolerated level.

Some of the bads (this opens up the next subject) hold threats to human life—situations causing traffic accidents or mining accidents—or pose threats to health, as in cigarette smoking or the application of pesticides. The number of lives lost or years of illness caused by threats of this kind can be reduced by expenditures for safety measures and by environmental constraints that inevitably increase costs of production to some extent. This fact allows and suggests another extension of the shadow price system: to place a value on human life, and on human health—a money value expressed in constant real dollars of some base year. Now the very idea of a dollar value on human life repels many people, many scientists, including in particular biological and medical scientists. It is an absolute anathema to politicians. However, we do indeed spend resources for saving human lives; we enforce speed limits, we impose public health measures, we have building safety codes backed up by inspection procedures. All these involve expenses to protect human life and health. The amount of the resources budgeted for these purposes is limited. A higher amount spent for protection would save more lives. But every next hundred thousand dollars so allocated will not save as many lives as the preceding hundred thousand dollars did: there is a kind of decreasing return to these expenditures in terms of lives saved. So we draw the line at some amount in our general practice. It is not any individual who does that. It is part of our institutions and procedures. We may find ourselves, if these procedures are a little haphazard, spending twice as much for lives saved to protect people from one risk as we do to protect them from some other risk. I had a conversation with a former official of the Department of Transportation who said the amount of money he had to lay out to do away with unguarded railway crossings did not save nearly as many lives, per thousand dollars spent, as some other uses he could find for the elimination of greater risks. In such cases more lives could be saved within the same budget by shifting some of the expenditure from a more costly to another less costly mode of protection. The following proposition is therefore a natural extension of the two preceding ones.

PROPOSITION A5. *The calculations of shadow prices can be further extended to valuations of existing human life and human health. Lives are implicitly valued by the additional cost of saving an additional life by protective measures or by medical care. Accurate valuation of both lives and health (years of healthy life), presupposes consistent policies to counter different threats to life and different impairments to health. Again, these values are relative to those of goods, and not absolute.*

Let me summarize the preceding five propositions in a sixth.

PROPOSITION A6. *The valuations, consisting of market and shadow prices, indicate in what ratio goods can be traded for, or produced instead of, other goods, can be converted into other goods (whether traded or not), and can be expended to reduce bads, and, indeed, to save lives or improve health. These valuations presuppose—and help achieve—both efficient operation of markets and efficient government decisions, that is, decisions that are mutually consistent as well as responsive to consumers' preferences and voters' desires.*

What is being aimed for by this line of reasoning is to assist Adam Smith's "invisible hand" that through the market guides business decisions, and supplement its action by the "visible hand" of government decisions that take environmental and other social effects into account in a quantitative way.

STEP B: THE VALUATION OF FUTURE GOODS AND SERVICES

So far I have only spoken of present, contemporary goods, services, and bads. Extending their valuation to future goods and bads is again something that economists engage in, and that has raised the eyebrows of many scientists. I resort again to a list of propositions in logical sequence.

PROPOSITION B1. *It is a technological fact that by consuming less this year and investing more in productive capital we can add more to future consumption than we take away from this year's consumption.*

This fact is not contested. We all benefit from the savings of earlier generations that have given us roads, buildings, factories, airports, and many other forms of durable capital.

PROPOSITION B2. *In a market economy this fact finds expression in a positive rate of return on capital investment.*

The issue here is not who receives the return on capital. There are important differences between different economic systems in the latter regard. In our market economy with private property, the ownership of capital rests with the private entrepreneur, or with the stockholders of corporations. In the latter case, the shareholder receives a return even though he does not have much of a voice in decisions. In the socialist economies the capital may be state owned and the return on capital may be spent or allocated in some other way at the direction of the government. There are many forms in between these two systems. The issue is not this range of institutional differences. The issue is that for good use of resources the use of capital also has to be accounted for, and brought into the calculation that guides which investments one makes and which one does not make. This requires that a charge for the use of the capital be included in the price of the product. Again, the charging of interest is almost an automatic standard procedure in a market economy. In the socialists economies it is in no way automatic, and it goes against the grain of the original thinking that led to the Soviet economic system, to the ground rules of it. However, the insight has also been gaining ground, slowly among Soviet economists and, to a larger degree and with a lesser delay, among policy makers in some other communist governments.

We can now formulate two propositions.

PROPOSITION B3. *The valuations that the propositions A deal with refer to a present period appropriately defined. Similar valuations applicable to any particular future period can be estimated as the shadow prices that reflect the anticipated cost of hypothetical or projected future technologies, the anticipated scarcity of future primary resource endowments, and future consumer preferences.*

PROPOSITION B4. *In order to merge all such present and future valuations into a single, all-inclusive system of intertemporal valuations, each set of evaluations bearing on any future period must be discounted to a general reference date in the present by a rate, a discount rate, that is simultaneously the real rate of return on capital and the rate that leads consumers to do the saving they do. In this system the "present values" of most future goods will be smaller and smaller as the time to which they refer lies further and further into the future.* (This reflects the technological and market facts noted in propositions B1 and B2.)

The following two formulas show a simple example of the elementary mathematics of discounting. Formula 1 defines the discounting procedure.

$$p_0 = \frac{p_t}{(1+r)^t} \tag{1}$$

Let p_t stand for the projected price, expressed in constant dollars, of some good in the year t. (By constant dollars I mean that inflation is not a factor here. Inflation has already been eliminated by dividing prices expressed in dollars of the year t by the proper price indices, for the year t, of the categories of goods involved.) So p_t, on the right in Formula 1, is the real dollar price in some future year t for a particular good. In order to compute the present value of that good, as seen from now but to be available only in the future, we divide the real dollar price p_t by a power $(1+r)^t$ of $(1+r)$, where r is the *discount rate*. Since r is positive, $1+r$ is larger than 1, and every time that t goes up by one year the *discount factor* $1/(1+r)^t$ on the right-hand side gets a little smaller. On the left we have the symbol p_0, which stands for the *present value,* as of year 0, of the prospect that the unit of the future good will be available at time t.

Formula 2 gives a numerical example.

$$p_0 = \frac{p_t}{1.06^{40}} \approx \frac{p_t}{10.3} \tag{2}$$

I have given to the discount rate the value of 6%, or 0.06. For t we look ahead 40 years, so I have computed for you, with the help of the pocket computer that Dr. McRostie lent me, what will be the present value of a good with a given future real price p_t. We have to divide that future price by about 10.3 in order to get the present value p_0.

This device is used not only in the planning of private business investments, but also for visualizing alternative futures of an entire economy. As an example of a very instructive application of the latter kind I wish to mention a study by my colleague William Nordhaus (1). He describes the current stage of history as "a transitory phase between dependence on cheap but scarce resources and dependence on more costly but abundant resources.'' The discounting of shadow prices of future goods is the principal analytical device. I regret that I shall not have time to give a proper description of the study here. However, I will indicate some links between the ideas of this study and some of our discussions in an earlier session.

If and when energy resources that are at the basis of present technologies come to run out, what will we have to fall back on? Well, a very natural proposal is to convert to solar energy. Dr. Commoner has already explained to us that solar energy could not fill the whole bill. Hence one might in addition look for other resources that also will last longer than those now in use. There are still oil shale and tar sands waiting to be developed, but perhaps at great environmental cost. There are a number of other possibilities to be considered, including nuclear fission, fusion, or combinations thereof. These considerations led Nordhaus to coin the term *backstop technology*, to refer to a single technology, or a mix of technologies, possessing a practically infinite resource base, and selected by the model calculation as the most economic solution that can serve us for an indefinite future.

If such a backstop technology can be identified, then to find the optimal path and duration of the transition to it involves the calculation of only a limited number of steps. For instance, under the deliberately unrealistic and artificial assumption of a competitive world market in oil with universal correct foresight into the future, he estimates the real-dollar shadow prices p_t of as yet unextracted oil in the Persian Gulf and North Africa (Nordhaus calls them ''royalties'') to be 18 cents per barrel in the year $t = 1970$, and 46 cents per barrel in the year $t = 1980$. In both cases these are prices based on the real value of the dollar in 1970. Comparison of these numbers with actual market prices (and noting the low cost of extraction) gives an idea of the market power of OPEC.

Note that the price of 46 cents for 1980 is an *un*discounted shadow price. Discounting the 1980 oil price back to 1970 with the rate $r = 0.10$ used in the model would bring it close to the 18 cents for 1970 oil, in seeming contradiction with the statement in parentheses at the end of proposition B4. The reason is that leaving oil untouched in the ground for 10 years is not a way to use the productivity of capital goods that could have been bought instead. To make this inaction acceptable to resource owners the competitive market must appreciate the real price of untouched oil at an annual rate numerically equal to the discount rate.

The mathematical reason for the low price figure for 1970 now becomes clear. It has to be as low as it is so that, by the time at which the backstop technology is phased in, the value of the energy contained in the last few barrels of oil to be extracted will have grown to the cost of the alternative energy henceforth to be obtained from the high-cost backstop technology.

Now, leaving aside the illustration of discounting by the example of the Nordhaus study, I summarize the role of business calculation implied in propositions B1 through B4 in the following.

PROPOSITION B5. *For development and production tasks that extend over time and are performed by business firms and corporations, the criterion of acceptability to the firm is profitability as estimated in the intertemporal value system read from the market, although subject to distortions from taxation, from monopoly, and from risk-taking aspects.*

The electorate may not want some of the outcomes that are favored by this criterion. In those cases national or international regulatory constraints or other forms of implementation will be looked for. I give some examples. One was inspired by Dr. Hardin: the protection of existing redwood forests and the replanting of denuded redwood forests. The public, through its decision-making channels, may care more for that than is revealed in the market. Another is the protection of animal species from extinction: there again the market does not work too well. Think of whales, for instance, where it is particularly important to note that if one animal, one female whale, is killed, then the potential progeny are thereby also eliminated. (Some other species are much more fertile than the whales and this last remark does perhaps not apply to the same extent.) One might then want, as an economist's idea, to place a penalty on the killing of whales that reflects the loss of future progeny. But if that is hard to implement, a more conventional procedure of protecting whales is by quota. I mention this then as an allocative task that the market does not perform but that can be and to some extent is performed better outside the market.

STEP C: PROJECTIONS FOR THE ENERGY SECTOR OF THE U.S. ECONOMY

Some projections of this type have been made recently in a study done for the National Research Council by the Committee of Nuclear and Alternative Energy Systems. That study had assigned to it a group of modelers of which I was the chairman. The modelers set themselves the task of putting together and comparing the answers given by different models to the same set of questions (2). Three of the models were optimization models that used the intertemporal valuation system that I have just described. In these models the discounted sum of future economic benefits minus costs was maximized, so as to simulate the behavior of a competitive market with long foresight. In order to take account of effects of environmental or other policies these studies also considered, besides a "base case," other cases in which further growth in either the use of coal or the use of nuclear processes was curtailed in one way or another. The principal purpose was to estimate how such policies would change the mix of energy technologies, the total cost of energy use, and ultimately the growth of gross national product. These projections have indicated that under plausible assumptions the response to one or the other of these curtailments, e.g., a curtailment in the growth of the use of coal or in the application of nuclear technology, could be absorbed. There is flexibility in the mix of future energy technologies, with only a moderate impact on the growth of GNP if these changes in technology mix are foreseen, are announced in advance as a policy objective, and are applied whenever the capital stock that is specific to a contracting technology turns over because of wear or obsolescence. I begin with a proposition that takes only the "goods" into account.

PROPOSITION C1. *Assuming a gradual phasing out of oil and gas, reliance on coal and on nuclear fission are found to be rather close substitutes in the economics of electricity generation. By present estimates central station solar electricity has a much higher capital cost, and greater energy storage problems.*

What happens if one brings in the adverse externalities? Their effects are still subject to great uncertainties already alluded to in my introduction. The following proposition expresses a tentative judgment rather than a logical conclusion.

PROPOSITION C2. *Because of considerable uncertainties about the environmental impacts from increased use of fossil fuels, and about the risks associated with the fuel cycles of the more advanced nuclear technologies, a flexible mix of major, approximately competitive, technologies would seem to be an acceptable strategy. At this point large scale solar electricity generation would seem to require large subsidies. These subsidies would have to be justified by the lesser environmental impacts and other risks solar energy might be shown to have.*

Another proposition describes the nature of the choices involved.

PROPOSITION C3. *The impact and risk problems associated with alternative energy technologies have now become international and indeed global in character. Their solution would have to be prepared by international scientific, technological, economic, and political consultation and negotiation.*

Again a few examples. I already mentioned the effects of increased CO_2 in the atmosphere. That is a global, not just a national, problem, and a potentially divisive one in that certain areas may benefit from the changes in climate that are expected, whereas others might suffer. There is also the problem of acid rain from the use of coal. I was told that in Norway and Sweden the acid rain that comes from the coal burned in the British Isles is a factor affecting their wildlife and agriculture. There is the proliferation problem: whether the handling of fuel reprocessing makes it possible either for terrorist groups, or for governments of countries not possessing nuclear weapons, to acquire weapons-grade materials. The awareness of this problem has increased and it is my feeling that in charting the nuclear future of the World one should either find new technologies and/or modify existing nuclear technologies in such a way that the risk of proliferation is thereby reduced—or else curtail and limit the use of these technologies. I do not use stronger language than that only because my technical understanding of these problems is limited.

The following proposition, for once, identifies a safe bet.

PROPOSITION C4. *Meanwhile, conservation of energy in industry, transportation, and domestic consumption should be pushed to the limits of its economic and environmental justification. In determining these limits the quantities and prices of all inputs to processes, whether they emphasize conservation or not, should be taken into account along with the saving of energy itself. In this comparison the proper price or shadow price of energy, current and future, is one crucial element. The prices of other inputs are also relevant and important, especially that of the use of capital.*

Once more, this is somewhat of a bone of contention between scientists and economists. Scientists have been brought up to think in terms of energy as the one pervasive entity throughout all of nature. That is, of course, so; the First Law of Thermodynamics testifies to that fact. But to the economist each form of energy is just one of many things, energy or not, that are extracted from mineral resources in some cases, that are produced by applying labor and capital in all cases, and are likely to require still other scarce inputs. An economist sees no reason why the energy cost of producing anything should not just be entered into all allocative calculations—assuming best use of resources—in the same way in which the costs of all other inputs are calculated. So to the scientist, the economist seems to dethrone energy from its august and unique position in the natural sciences. There is no such intent. However, for economic calculation there does not seem to be any reason to follow a different procedure for energy inputs on that account; therefore, calculations that consider only inputs and outputs of energy in one form or another are regarded by the economist as insufficient and, indeed, misleading.

STEP D: MORE ON THE VALUATION OF HUMAN LIVES AND HEALTH

Problems have arisen, at least speculatively, that would require a choice between the protection of human life existing now and that of life existing in a distant future. Examples are three alternative methods for disposing of radioactive waste materials from nuclear reactors. One is underground disposal in the best-suited geological stratum available. The risk that may be associated with that—and I have no opinion on its numerical importance—is that ultimately, although the less long-lived radioactive components have already decayed, the plutonium that is present, with its longer half-life than most of the others, will still be there for a long time and may by some cracks or other corrosion of the containers get into the groundwater. This is a very long term risk. A second alternative, which I would regard as a medium term risk is to hold the materials above ground for reprocessing and for inclusion to the extent possible in the nuclear fuel input to a breeder reactor if and when available. In this way, a substantial fraction of the plutonium nuclei would cease to exist as such much sooner. The case for that option may be a good one. Again, I just mention this as a possibility without a technical opinion of my own, but if there is such a possibility I would call it a medium term risk. The third alternative is more in the science fiction category. Why not place the nuclear waste materials on board a rocket and then shoot it out into space and into the sun? The principal risk in that is immediate; that the rocket might fail and that the materials would be released into the atmosphere or onto the surface of the earth.

Now in all these cases a probability weight needs to be attached to the possible harm that might result. After that is done the principal difference between the three methods is the time at which, in the future, the possible impacts occur. At this point ethical reflection would suggest that equal weight be given to protection of existing lives regardless of whether these are lives existing in the present, in the near future, or in the distant future. However, the present value of goods in the distant future is likely to be quite small by the calculation I have given an example of. It is true that for various reasons we can expect the ratio of the value of future life to the value of future goods to be higher than it is at the present, but I do not think we can expect it to be so much higher that we could avoid a contradiction or an inconsistency in the valuation of future life between two calculations—one via the goods that may be spent in the future to protect life, the other one according to the ethical principle I have just advanced. So here I express this puzzle in my most difficult proposition.

PROPOSITION D1. *The likely inconsistency between the ratio of the value of lives existing in the future to that of future goods, as seen from the present, and as seen in the future, calls for deep and soul-searching thought.*

Leaving this puzzle aside I go on to a type of decision affecting human life that has not yet been discussed. I start with the following.

PROPOSITION D2. *The creation of new human life is by no means exclusively an economic decision, although it also has economic aspects for the deliberate decision maker.*

However, the scale on which this decision is made has important economic consequences for a nation and, indeed, for the world as a whole. It is not proposed here to calculate a numerical value for not yet existing lives. However, the historical record of the developed countries shows by and large a decrease in the rate of population growth as income per capita rises. This was, for instance, also emphasized in conversations I was privileged to have with Professor Herrera of the Bariloche Foundation in Argentina. He felt that the main route of population control to be relied on in the future would be to bring up the level of income. This observation suggests a programmatic proposition.

PROPOSITION D3. *It is a question for empirical analysis and pooled judgment whether or not the carrying capacities of the respective countries and of the world as a whole between them permit the process of rising income and diminishing population growth to evolve into a stationary population without large famines or epidemics on the way.*

This is my last-but-one proposition, and it leads me to address a few questions to Dr. Hardin. In the materials submitted to the Conference by Dr. Hardin or in his recent book *The Limits of Altruism*, I have not found references to projections of future net growth of population, of per capita food supply, and of other income that would make it possible to throw light on this empirical question. Neither have I found a formal definition of the important concept of carrying capacity, that is, a definition in terms of a model that has quantitative components that would allow the defining of future carrying capacity and the estimation thereof based on explicitly stated assumptions. In particular, in the materials he has given us, I have found no quantitative discussion and assessment of the probable outcome of the race between population growth and technical advances in resource extraction, in the production of goods and services, and, in particular, of energy, again under various alternative assumptions, because we cannot be too sure of any one set of assumptions. I hope Dr. Hardin will share with us his thinking in these matters.

I express a conjecture on future population policies in my very last proposition.

PROPOSITION D6. *So far policies directly aimed at constraining population growth have been formulated and applied in only a few countries. It is conceivable but not a certainty that such policies will become more widespread, and will then also become a matter of international discussion and perhaps implicit negotiation—along with more explicit negotiation and agreement concerning global energy and environmental problems.*

This is my conjecture about possible future developments.

REFERENCES

1. Nordhaus, W. 1973. The allocation of energy resources. Brookings Papers on Economic Activity, pp. 529–570. Brookings Institute, Washington, D.C.
2. Energy Modeling for an Uncertain Future. Supporting Paper 2 of the Study of Nuclear and Alternative Energy Systems. National Academy of Sciences, Washington, D.C., 1978.

chapter 4
An Ecolate View of the Human Predicament

Garrett Hardin

How should rich nations respond to the demands of poor nations? Economist Jan Tinbergen, arguing for a redistribution of the world's wealth, has said:

> Apparently you cannot convince nations that they should assist others voluntarily. But people should realize that if no solution is found, the future looks rather bleak. If the rich countries will not share their wealth, the poor people of the world will come and take it for themselves (1).

Tinbergen presents two arguments for the redistribution of wealth, one implicitly based on moral grounds, the other an explicitly practical argument that we should bow gracefully to the inevitable. I challenge both arguments.

The influential anarchist-communist (a common hybrid, by the way) Pierre-Joseph Proudhon (1809–1865), said flatly that "Property is theft." This assertion has led in our day to the conclusion that *need creates right,* catalyzing the creation of such international redistributional devices as easy credit banks, and demands for world food reserves and a "New International Economic Order." The United States, like every rich nation, stands to suffer direct losses from redistribution, but that is hardly an adequate reason for rejecting such proposals if in fact they might achieve their primary goal (sharing the wealth) as well as their more important secondary goal of creating a peaceful and stable world order. It is my contention that redistribution will do neither. Poverty can be shared, but it is doubtful if wealth can. Although universal poverty might, when achieved, make high technology war impossible, the intermediary process of impoverishment would trigger the very kinds of military action we hope to avoid. I will return to these practical matters later. First let me take up the theoretical reasons for rejecting redistribution as a cure for the poverty of nations.

I think we can find no better guide to inquiry than an aphorism of August Comte (1798–1857): "The Intellect should always be the servant of the Heart, and never its slave." Comte was the first proponent of "Positivism," a philosophical approach generally regarded as "hard-nosed." Note, however, that the philosopher gave first place to the Heart. Values are paramount: it is the role of the Intellect to find a way of achieving what the Heart desires. But the Heart, by definition, can scarcely be expected to be very intellectual; its uninstructed impulses may, in fact, be counterproductive of its goals. The task of Intellect is to examine these impulses and, in its role of faithful executive officer, restructure them productively.

The most popular policies now proposed for diminishing poverty among nations are counterproductive in that they all fail to take account of what I have called "the tragedy of the commons." In embryonic form the idea can be found as far back as Aristotle: "That which is common to the greatest number gets the least amount of care. Men pay most attention to what is their own: they care less for what is common" (2). A true statement, but not forceful enough; by neglecting to emphasize and quantify the mechanisms of choice Aristotle failed to reveal the tragedy of the process. In 1968 I attempted to rectify this shortcoming in the following words (3):

> The tragedy of the commons develops in this way. Picture a pasture open to all. It is to be expected that each herdsman will try to keep as many cattle as possible on the commons. Such an arrangement may work reasonably satisfactorily for centuries because tribal wars, poaching, and disease keep the numbers of both man and beast well below the carrying capacity of the land. Finally, however, comes the day of reckoning, that is, the day when the long-desired goal of social stability becomes a reality. At this point, the inherent logic of the commons remorselessly generates tragedy.
>
> As a rational being, each herdsman seeks to maximize his gain. Explicitly or implicitly, more or less consciously, he asks, "What is the utility *to me* of adding one more animal to my herd?" This utility has one negative and one positive component.
>
> 1) The positive component is a function of the increment of one animal. Since the herdsman receives all the proceeds from the sale of the additional animals, the positive utility is nearly + 1.
>
> 2) The negative component is a function of the additional overgrazing created by one more animal. Since, however, the effects of overgrazing are

shared by all the herdsmen, the negative utility for any particular decision-making herdsman is only a fraction of -1.

Adding together the component partial utilities, the rational herdsman concludes that the only sensible course for him to pursue is to add another animal to his herd. And another; and another.... But this is the conclusion reached by each and every rational herdsman sharing a commons. Therein is the tragedy. Each man is locked into a system that compels him to increase his herd without limit—in a world that is limited. Ruin is the destination toward which all men rush, each pursuing his own best interest in a society that believes in the freedom of the commons. Freedom in a commons brings ruin to all.

As a result of discussions carried out during the past decade I now suggest a better wording of the central idea: *Under conditions of overpopulation, freedom in an unmanaged commons brings ruin to all.* When there is no scarcity, as is the case in a pioneer community with ample resources, an unmanaged commons may in fact be the best distributional device since it avoids the costs of management (4). It must be pleasant to live in such an uncrowded world; but when shortages develop the prospect of tragedy has to be faced. Even with crowding and its consequent scarcity, the experience of such religious communes as the Hutterites shows that formal management does not necessarily have to be invoked if the informal power of shame is available. Apparently shame works only if the community does not exceed about 150 people; beyond that number this informal control is not effective enough to prevent "freeloading" and the drift toward the tragedy of the commons (5).

In larger communities, under conditions of scarcity or overpopulation—two words for the same situation—either the commons must be broken up or it must be managed. We may speak of *privatism* when the commons is broken up into units of private property, and *socialism* when it is retained as one piece and managed by agents of the community, i.e., by bureaucrats. The name *commonism* has been proposed (6) for the system in which the commons is *not* managed, but is freely available to all. (The older term "communism" is unfortunately ambiguous: it sometimes refers to commonism—as here defined—and sometimes to socialism. One suspects that some who use the older term cherish its ambiguity.)

The comparative merits of privatism and socialism need not concern us here (4, 7). Depending on other factors either privatism or socialism *can* work, more or less; but, under populous conditions, commonism cannot possibly work. The aim of commonism was neatly expressed by Karl Marx in 1875: "From each according to his ability, to each according to his needs'' (8). Marx did no more than express very well what most Christians regard as their ideal—which is ironic, considering the low opinion Marx had of religion (''the opium of the people''). The commons of English pastureland is no longer of great practical importance, although 600,000 marginal hectares are still being maltreated in this way (9). More important are numerous other examples throughout the world. Let me cite a few. The desertification of the Mediterranean basin, particularly the southern and eastern portions, is due to a large extent to the grazing and browsing of goats in the commons; so also in Iran. These are old evils. Not so with the galloping deforestation of Nepal, which dates from the 1950s when the government put an end to the feudal control of land, thus opening up the forests to fuel-hungry people (10). In the U.S., grazing lands in the national forests are nominally socialistically controlled, but the U.S. Forest Service is so obsequious to private herdsmen that the governance is de facto commonistic. That the oceanic fisheries are a commons, and that they are headed for disaster, is now widely recognized; a slight improvement in the situation has been created by the recent extension of national rights out to the 200-mile limit. The assertion of national privatism will have little effect on wide-ranging species, but it may help others, provided the area protected against international encroachment is not commonized nationally.

Although a commons tends toward a tragic outcome, the seriousness of the danger depends on quantitative factors. The common wealth of the atmosphere as an absorptive resource for pollutants was not a matter of great concern so long as population and industrial activities were at a low enough level. Now the situation is different. Since privatism is hardly an option for the air and waters of the world, socialistic or semisocialistic regulation is called for. Within national boundaries we know something about the requirements of good management (11), even though we are often unwilling to meet these requirements, but how we are to secure the international cooperation of many sovereign states is still a mystery.

The more crowded the world becomes, the less tolerable are the commons. There is now a large literature pointing this out, yet still old commons survive and new ones are created (12). Part of the pathology is due to the fact that short term gains generally weigh more heavily in decision making than do long term losses. Mr. Micawber is always with us: ''Something will turn up,'' say the technological optimists, among whom the economists are preeminent. We are especially tempted to create a new commons when the short term effect is a diminution of suffering. Thus we created a World Bank for making ''soft loans,'' most of which will probably ultimately go into default and have to be covered by rich governments, principally by the U.S. (The word "loan" becomes a euphemism for the privilege of drawing on a commons.) So also do we move spasmodically toward a world food bank on which overpopulated countries can draw according to need. It should be obvious that a world food bank governed by the Marxist-Christian principle is a commons headed for tragedy (13), and yet this destructive distribution system has many supporters. What has gone wrong with the world, that is Intellect could be so much the slave of its unthinking Heart?

At the deepest level our problem is an educational one. In the Western world literacy has been taken as almost synonymous with education; yet a generation ago some insightful person (I don't know who), asserting that literacy is not enough, said that we need also *numeracy*, the ability to handle numbers and the habit of demanding them. A merely literate person may raise no question when a journalist speaks of "the inexhaustible wealth of the sea," or "the infinite resources of the earth." The numerate person, by contrast, asks for figures and rates. Perhaps it takes more imagination to think with figures than with ambiguous, airy generalizations, but the mind can be helped by graphs, which Bishop Oresme invented in the 14th century. Graphing is a precious resource of numeracy. What a commentary it is on the slow progress of education that today's leading journals, generally referred to as "intellectual"—*Harpers, Atlantic Monthly, Kenyon Review*, and the like—never use graphs to illuminate ideas. ["Have you noticed," asked the mathematician G. H. Hardy, "how the word 'intellectual' is used nowadays? There seems to be a new definition which certainly doesn't include Rutherford or Eddington or Dirac or Adrian or me. It does seem rather odd, don't y'know" (14).] Six centuries have passed since Oresme—six centuries of glorious progress in scientifically enriching our vision of the world: is it not time that our self-styled "intellectuals" become numerate as well as literate?

I think a good case can be made for a third level of education, the level of *ecolacy*. This is the level at which a person achieves a working understanding of the complexity of the world, of the ways in which each quasi-stable state gives way to other quasi-stable states as time passes. The three levels of education can be epitomized by three questions:

Literacy—*What is the appropriate word?*
Numeracy—*How much/how many?*
Ecolacy—*And then what?*

The basic insight of the ecolate citizen is that the world is a complex of systems so intricately interconnected that we can seldom be very confident that a proposed intervention in this system of systems will produce the consequences we want. Rachel Carson's *Silent Spring* (15) is a monument to this insight; so also are the many contributions in Farvar and Milton's *The Careless Technology* (16). Like the sorcerer's apprentice, we learn the hard way that *we can never do merely one thing* (17, 18). In building the High Aswan Dam engineers intended only to produce more water and more electricity. They succeeded in their expressed goal, but at what cost? Deprived of the fertilizing silt of the Nile floodwaters the sardine population of the eastern Mediterranean has diminished by 97% (19). The rich delta of the Nile, which increased in area for thousands of years, is now being rapidly eroded away by the Mediterranean because the Nile is depositing no more silt at its mouth. Until Aswan, the yearly flooding of riverine farms added 1 mm of rich silt to the land annually; now that the floods are stopped the previous silt is piling up behind the dam, diminishing its capacity. Soon the poor Nile farmers will have to buy artificial fertilizer (if they have the money). Moreover, irrigation without flooding always salinates the soil: in a few hundred years (at most) the Nile valley, which has been farmed continuously for 5000 years, will have to be abandoned. In the meantime year-round irrigation favors snails and the debilitating disease they carry, schistosomiasis; control of this disease is now much more expensive.

How did all this come about? A not inconsiderable cause of disasters like this is our semantic befuddlement. We speak of "developing" a backward country: the implicit metaphor is biological. A tadpole develops into a frog because this individual-historic change is programmed into the genetic code of the creature. But human history has no discernible program. (Human will could negate it if it had. Q.E.D.) The belief that history has a program is a fallacy that Karl Popper calls "historicism," the moral dangers of which he ably demonstrates (20). "The future," as the engineer-philosopher Dennis Gabor has said (21), "cannot be predicted, but futures can be invented." When a rich country intervenes in the affairs of a poor country it is not acting as a mere midwife, facilitating a development that is inevitable anyway. The intervener, knowingly or not, is attempting to invent the future of the client. If the word "responsibility" is taken in its ordinary meaning, a rich country is surely responsible for whatever good or ill follow from its presumably well intentioned interventions.

The possibility of causing more harm than good seldom enters the mind of an international intervener. The intervener in Egypt—the U.S.S.R., as it happened, but it would have been the U.S., had we not earlier had a falling out with Nasser—no doubt viewed the goal as one of working toward a maximum of electricity production, or irrigation water (or both). The goal of maximizing a single variable is woven into the fabric of engineering, and it has long seemed an innocent goal. The political scientist William Ophuls, however, calls on us to reexamine this assumption in terms of a bit of modern folk wisdom that has been called Ophuls' Axiom: *Nature abhors a maximum* (22). Survival of any system depends on a subtle and incompletely understood balance of many variables. Maximizing one is almost sure to alter the balance in an unfavorable way. So complex is every natural system that the cascade of consequences started by an ill-advised maximization of a single variable may take years, or even generations, to work itself out. This is the reason why proponents of intervention find it so easy to close their eyes to the consequences of their meddling. The goals of energy maximization, optimum capital utilization, personal utility maximalization, and optimal resource depletion all become suspect under Ophuls' Axiom.

In the ecolate view of the world, time has no stop: every well meant proposal must be challenged by the question, "And then what?" Refusal to meet this challenge is the commonest cause of the failure of social reforms. Slum clearance, urban redevelopment, and most welfare programs have been generally counterproductive of their goals because their proponents, largely literate and not ecolate in their thinking, did not subject their plans to the acid test of "And then what?"

Wittgenstein once remarked that "Philosophy is a battle against the bewitchment of our intelligence by means of language" (23). In the realm that we might call "international welfare economics" two particularly bewitching terms are "world hunger" and "shortages." It is essential that we challenge these usually unchallenged terms if we are to separate fact from interpretation.

There are numerous pockets of hunger and poverty scattered throughout the world. Does that fact justify speaking of "world hunger" or "world poverty"? Earthquakes, too, are widely scattered throughout the world, but we do not speak of "the world earthquake problem." Earthquakes are local problems, to be handled by local means, e.g., the enforcement of building codes locally. What would be gained by insisting that all the world be concerned with (for example) California's earthquake problems? A large bureaucracy would be created, which would employ many people—but is that sufficient excuse for globalizing earthquake problems? Would globalizing the problems diminish the damage of earthquakes or reduce the cost of dealing with them? We, the inheritors of the wisdom of Parkinson (24), do not think so.

To speak of "world hunger" and "world poverty" is to globalize hunger and poverty problems—that is, to imply that they must be dealt with by the distributional system of the commons. It may be compassionate to say, ". . . to each according to his needs," but it is not wise, because "each," being a biological organism will, if its needs are well supplied, breed more "each's," thus increasing global needs without limit, in a world of finite resources. The phrases "world hunger" and "world poverty" tend to create in the auditor an unconscious commitment to a commons. Since the system of the commons is disastrous under conditions of scarcity we should eschew the terms "world hunger" and "world poverty."

The idea of scarcity also needs examining, if we are not to be bewitched by words. The problem of poverty is almost invariably seen as one of *shortages*—shortages of supply. But note: poverty can just as logically be seen as a problem of *longages*—longages of demand (25). Given these two equally logical modes of expression, why do people invariably choose the first as a guide to action, scarcely even mentioning the second? This is a deep question. The usual choice is tragic because the well documented conclusion from ecology is that only the second approach—attempting to diminish the longage of demand—has any chance of succeeding in the long run. The ecological theory of matching supply to demand is grounded in the concept of "carrying capacity."

In explaining the meaning and properties of carrying capacity we will first look at nonhuman animals. This approach does not deny special status to the human animal; experience shows, however, that it is easier to be objective about animals than about ourselves, particularly when the problem is as psychologically threatening as the problem of human poverty. I investigate first the implications of carrying capacity for other animals; then I look at how the conclusions thus reached have to be modified when we apply them to the human predicament.

The carrying capacity of a portion of the environment for a population is a matter of central importance in any species that we propose to exploit, either as game animals or domestic animals. Several characteristics of carrying capacity merit discussion.

1. The environment is variable from season to season, year to year, and perhaps over longer periods; momentary carrying capacity likewise varies.
2. If policy is to be based on a unique estimate of the carrying capacity, the figure chosen should be neither the maximum nor the average: it should be somehwere near the minimum (at least the minimum for the year; perhaps for longer periods). Why? For the following reason.
3. Transgressing the carrying capacity for one period lowers the carrying capacity thereafter, perhaps starting a downward spiral toward zero.

David Klein's classic study of the reindeer on St. Matthew Island illustrates the point (26). In 1944 a population of 29 animals was moved to the island, without the corrective feedback (negative feedback) of such predators as wolves and human hunters. In 19 years the population swelled to 6,000 and then "crashed" in 3 years to a total of 41 females and one male, all in miserable condition. Klein estimates that the primeval carrying capacity of the island was about 5 deer per square kilometer. At the population peak there were 18 per square kilometer. After the crash there were only 0.126 animals per square kilometer *and even this was probably too many* once the island was largely denuded of lichens. Recovery of lichens under zero population conditions takes decades; with a continuing resident population of reindeer it may never occur. Transgressing the carrying capacity of St. Matthew Island reduced its carrying capacity by at least 97.5 percent. It is facts like these—repeated over and over again in game management experience—that justify the ecolate game manager in viewing carrying capacity as partaking of the sacred. I do not think it is going too far to assert and defend the *sanctity of the carrying capacity.*

4.   How, then, are we to view the concept of "the sanctity of life"? Mere mention of this makes us think of the human situation and our defenses are immediately aroused. I must emphasize, therefore, that we are for the moment concerned only with nonhuman animals (although we will later examine the human situation). In this limited context the following is unquestionably true: *In game management the concept of "the sanctity of life" is intolerable.* The reason is simple. Once the population has reached the carrying capacity of the environment, the cherishing of each and every individual life will result in a transgression of the carrying capacity and a subsequent degradation of carrying capacity. Cherishing individual lives in the short run diminishes the number of lives in the long run. It also diminishes the quality of life and increases the pain of living it. In terms of its implicit goal—maximizing the number of lives and decreasing pain—*the concept of the sanctity of life is counterproductive.* To achieve its goal the concept of the sanctity of life must give precedence to the concept of the sanctity of carrying capacity.

[This analysis also throws light on the operational meaning of Comte's statement that the Intellect should be the servant, not the slave, of the Heart. In effect, the Intellect says to the Heart, "You are on the right track in speaking of the sanctity of life, but the verbalization of your goal has proven injudicious. You must accept another wording that takes account of the passage of time, the needs of posterity, and the conflict of short and long term goals. Paradoxical though it may seem to you (dear Heart!) sanctifying carrying capacity will, in fact, better serve the end you seek when you speak of the sanctity of life. To achieve the end you want you must give up the intuitive ideal with which you began.''']

5.   We must not fail to note the bearing of ecological knowledge on the concept of waste. When the consequences of error in the estimation of a limiting figure are very serious the ''prudent man'' keeps well away from the limit. Engineers have long recognized this principle: thus it is that the traffic permitted over a bridge is kept well below the best estimate of the possible limit. The legal limit of a bridge creates unused capacity. Do we apply the term ''waste'' to capacity that is unused? We do not. Similarly the legal maximum for a well managed population of animals should leave some food unused—which we should not call ''waste.''

The implications of carrying capacity are clear for nonhuman populations. Can they be applied without change to our own species? Before we can answer this we must examine two concepts in detail: technology, and the quality of life.

Technology has permitted the human species to increase carrying capacity greatly in the past, and promises to continue to do so for some time in the future. A qualification needs to be mentioned: not all aspects that we regard as part of the carrying capacity for human beings can be increased to the same extent. We can increase the amount of food energy we extract from the environment, but how do we increase the amount of wilderness for recreation or the extent of lonely beaches and wild rivers needed for the renewal of the spirit? If several variables are included in the reckoning of carrying capacity, maximizing the one that can be most easily maximized, and keying population size to that variable, will necessarily diminish the per capita allotment of all other goods. There are those who claim we shall some day have an infinite amount of energy at our disposal. Before we set out to make that dream a reality we should review Fremlin's demonstration that an unlimited energy supply *without population control* would, in fact, cause the extinction of the human race (27).

In the human realm the concept of carrying capacity is inseparable from the problem of the quality of life. If we want to eat meat the carrying capacity of the land is less than if we are satisfied with plant food only. If we want everyone to enjoy automobiles, airplanes, and central heating we must settle for a rather small population.

A particularly bothersome problem is raised by the observation that different human populations now enjoy different standards of living.

Mahbub Ul Haq, a World Bank economist, recently pointed out that a child born in a rich country will consume 20 to 40 times as much resources as a child born in a poor country (29). And, he says, "the very small population increases in the rich world put about eight times the pressure on world resources [that] the very large increases in the poor world [will]." To statements like this (and they have been made often) we must reply sharply, *So what?*—and then stay for an answer.

If the moral is, rich people should stop reproducing, we must ask: *And then what?* Whatever world resources might be freed in this way would soon be completely absorbed by the multiplying poor. So instead of a world divided between rich and poor we would soon have a world of poor people only. Is that what we want?

Or is the moral this: that the rich should reduce their per capita resource use to the level of the poor? If so, this is merely another way of achieving universal poverty. Again we must ask, is that what we want?

Does God give a prize for the maximum number of people? One might think so, to judge from statements made by latter-day Puritans who seem willing to reduce the standard of living everywhere in the world to a bare bones level. Temperence is admirable, but do we really want to reintroduce the sumptuary laws of the past in order to create a straitened lifestyle for all?

Notice that the concept of the commons is implicit in Haq's use of the term "world resources" for resources that are, in fact, distributed very spottily around the globe. "World resources" is an echo of Proudhon's "Property is theft." Commonizing the discontinuously distributed resources of the world will, of course, evoke the usual tragedy (unless we can bring about the miracle of a single World State). Why, then, are statements like Haq's so fashionable?

The answer, I think, is to be found in envy and the fear of envy. Envy moves the poor to demand commonization of resources; fear of envy causes some of the rich to accede. The discussion of envy, as the sociologist Helmut Schoeck has shown (30), is under a considerable taboo, so the word is seldom heard. Instead the talk is of justice (31). Love of justice is fine—but not if it leads to the establishment of a commons in a world ruled by scarcity. No truly ecolate thinker can agree with the motto of the Holy Roman Emperor, Ferdinand I (1503–1564): *Fiat justitia et pereat mundus*—"Let justice be done, though the world perish."

That we have a higher regard for human life than we do for the life of other living things requires no apology. But the higher value placed on human life calls for no change in our previous ethical conclusion, namely, that the sanctity of the carrying capacity takes precedence over the sanctity of life. Once we accept this conclusion we discover that contemporary population/environment problems are even more terrible than we previously thought. Erik Eckholm in *Losing Ground* has painted a graphic picture of the tragedy now overtaking the people in the tropical highlands (32). The energy that they need for cooking their food they get from burning the wood of the trees around them. In addition, some highlanders make charcoal to heat little braziers in winter or to sell to outsiders, as the Kashmiri do to Indians. Modern medicine and more food have enabled highland populations to outstrip the productivity of their lands for timber. As people deforest the land the soil washes off, making reforestation all but impossible on steep slopes. Once transgressed, carrying capacity is progressively degraded. Soil lost to the highlands clogs irrigation systems in the lowlands—often of another nation—and silts up lakes behind the dams, thus diminishing their useful life. The loss of water-holding capacity in the highlands causes floods in the lowlands to peak higher and faster, destroying many more human lives and much more property. Only 10% of the world's population lives in the highlands, but, as Eckholm points out, the harm of their overpopulation affects 30% of the world's people.

What can be done? Conceivably rich countries might ship oil and oil-burners to some 400 million highlanders—but how likely is such generosity now that the rich perceive the "energy shortage" as their major problem? To supply the poor with a great variety of solar heaters and cookers would require an immense diversion of capital. Moreover, do we possess the anthropological expertise to bring about the necessary change in folkways? As an alternate solution, people in adjacent lowlands might offer to take in some 200 million immigrants from the highlands: but the lowlanders are themselves mostly wretchedly poor—think of Bangladesh, and the Bihar in India. Again there is an anthropological question: How can one gently uproot a people and persuade them to live a different life elsewhere? Rich nations could more easily afford to take in hundreds of millions of immigrants, but in that case the problem of ethnic adjustment would be even more severe.

The unrealistic character of these proposals is obvious. I think most people, untrained though they be in ecology, unconsciously weigh such proposals in an ecolate way, asking *And then what?* After we transport the surplus poor to other areas, or ship extra energy into their homelands, will not the present rate of population increase continue unabated? Such populations now typically increase at 3% per year, which means that their populations potentially increase nineteenfold per century. It is insanity to view poverty in such circumstances as a problem of shortages: it is a long-age problem. And we don't know what to do about it.

It is time to face the music. Discussing the human predicament in terms of carrying capacity—a concept that originated in animal husbandry and game management—inevitably raises the suspicion that someone is about to propose treating human beings like cattle or wild animals. When a herd of animals is overpopulated we do not hesitate to liquidate the excess, that is, to kill them. Anyone who speaks of carrying capacity in connection with human population problems is suspected of following the lead of Nazi Germany or contemporary Cambodia. We must not repress this suspicion: we must bring it out into the open so that we can discuss the human predicament frankly.

At the barren and heartless level of pure logic a game management solution should work for humans as it does for other animals: but the Heart won't stand for it. The Heart, too, is an ecologist, and asks *And then what?* The liquidation of excess lives might be sincerely proposed as a solution for a temporary crisis; unfortunately every act potentially sets a precedent. Liquidation can be both infectious and addictive. It can bring into existence a positive feedback system that is destructive both ethically and politically. It can destabilize society, bringing on a new Dark Age. The ecolate Heart knows this.

But in rejecting a policy of liquidition we must not forget the fact that led us to consider it, namely, the primacy of the concept of carrying capacity in the theory of all populations, animal or human. In the human situation technology can increase the carrying capacity of the environment, but it cannot do so at an arbitrarily rapid rate, and there may be practical limits to what technology can do. Some optimists say that technology can always raise the carrying capacity of the human environment faster than the growth of human population. In some theoretical framework this may be true (for a while), but in the existing political and economic framework (which is resistant to change) it is hard to defend the thesis that the present rate of population increase is nothing to worry about. Justifiably we complain of the population-related ills of poverty, pollution, inflation, and unemployment. We should suspect that the carrying capacity of our environment has already been transgressed.

It was one of the less happy consequences of Malthus's celebrated essay that it focused people's attention on food. But man does not live by food alone. A humane definition of an acceptable standard of living includes much more than mere food. A humane and prudent man strongly suspects that the carrying capacity of our environment—as defined by aspirations, technology, and political realities—has already been transgressed. If you doubt this ask yourself the following questions. Is the supply of such natural amenities as wilderness and quiet countryside now increasing? Is the threat to endangered species a figment of the imagination? Is the cost of controlling pollution decreasing? Does inflation show signs of disappearing? Can we forget about unemployment? Is the proportion of the world's peoples living under democratic governments now on the increase? Is our elbow room for political maneuvering to meet crises increasing?

We must never forget the role choice plays in defining carrying capacity in the human situation. The desired standard of living and the inferred carrying capacity are inversely related. Given a high standard of living and a low carrying capacity, transgressing the carrying capacity lowers the standard of living. The loss may be painful but it is not lethal. But when a large population existing at a minimal standard of living transgresses the carrying capacity of its environment there is only one direction for both the population and the standard of living to go and that is *down*. Then is the history of the St. Matthew Island Reindeer translated into human terms. Human dignity is degraded; human lives are lost.

What shall we do when carrying capacity is transgressed by a human population that is still growing? Obviously population growth needs first to be brought to a halt, and then reversed (for a while). How can this be accomplished if we reject (as we should) the policy of liquidation? Fortunately we have a model of a better alternative in the realm of business practice and that is the practice of *attrition*.

Before seeing how this idea might be adapted to population control let us see how it operates in an area where it is already accepted. It frequently happens that an organization—a business concern or an educational establishment—finds that its supply of employees amounts to overpopulation in terms of a realistic estimate of future opportunities. If a business firm is desperately competing with other firms in the same business the management may have to resort to the sort of liquidation we call firing. If, however, business competition is not too severe, or if the concern is an educational one living off the commons of tax funds, a reduction of the employee population can be brought about by attrition, i.e., by not refilling (for a while) vacancies created by normal retirements, deaths, and resignations. Attrition is slower than liquidation; it is also gentler and more acceptable. It takes into account the so-called secondary effects— which are not really secondary—of the mode of population reduction employed. Positive utilities are balanced against negative utilities. In principle, there could be an economic theory of attrition, although I don't suppose it yet exists. Such a theory would tell us what the optimal path of attrition is, i.e., the path that is the least pessimal.

Attrition theory should be as much a part of social and economic education as the theory and practice of retreat is in the education of the military. Just as death is part of life so also do failures and defeats partake of the essence of progress, although our persistent belief in Providence usually blinds us to what we regard as the darker side of existence. But is it really darker? No defeat is total except in terms of a particular partial goal. Superficial thinkers hold that the proper response to defeat is always "Try harder!," but it is sometimes more rational to redirect our efforts toward other, more realistic goals.

The application of attrition to population control should be obvious. An excess of population does *not* call for liquidation; it can be corrected for by *attrition through diminished fertility*. The normal, inescapable death rate will reduce population size if we see to it that the fertility rate is sufficiently reduced. We don't need to kill anybody; we just have to make sure that new bodies are not produced at quite so fast a rate. For instance, a program might be adopted of allowing only one birth for each two deaths. Of course, negative population growth will alter the age distribution of the population, thus affecting economic and social processes. The cultural changes required to produce population control will themselves have consequences. It will not be easy to find the least pessimal rate of change, but this should be regarded as a proper task of an as yet unborn theory of attrition.

In the past, what we have called "foreign aid" has almost wholly sidestepped the central problem of carrying capacity; its accomplishments have been equivocal. By any reasonable standard, 2500 millions of the world's peoples are now poor. The rate of growth of the poor populations has risen fairly steadily during the entire period of foreign aid (1950 to the present) from about 1% per year at the beginning to nearly 3% at the present time, and the rate operates on an ever larger base of impoverished populations. Current rumors of a significant decrease in the rate are without factual foundation.

To the list of clichés that have bewitched our intelligence during the past generation we must add the term "foreign aid." When Congress votes billions of dollars to be spent in foreign countries all that we can objectively say about the enterprise is that it is *foreign intervention*. Calling it aid is prejudicial and will interfere with our observing the true effects of our actions. There is a large and growing body of evidence that past foreign interventions have, on balance, been less than aidful (see references 16 and 33–39). Aidfulness must be proved, not assumed; until it is we should use only the nonprejudicial label, foreign intervention.

Whenever we are tempted to try to cure the economic illnesses of other nations we should remember the cautionary words of Molière (1622–1673) with regard to the physical medicine of his time: "Nearly all men die of their remedies and not of their illnesses" (40). It was for this reason that wise physicians before the 20th century followed the rule, *Primum non nocere*—"First do no harm." Many an early physician gained a justifiably great reputation by administering nothing but placebos. Now that we have penicillin, physicians need not be quite so cautious; but the profession of foreign intervention has yet to find its penicillin.

Shutting our eyes as we do to the harm that foreign intervention does, it is natural for us to casually assume that our motivation for intervening is purely philanthropic; but I think one can make a plausible case that this is not so. It is not unreasonable to suspect that foreign aid programs are merely the latest manifestation of a national arrogance that exhibited itself earlier in the phrase "manifest destiny," which in 1845 was used by Americans to justify stealing Texas from Mexico (41). This act we now admit was one of military imperialism. But what about the words with which President Truman launched "Point Four," later to be called foreign aid? In 1949 Truman called on America to "embark on a bold new program" to rescue "more than half of the people of the world. . . living in conditions approaching misery" (42, 43). Thirty intervening years (and billions of dollars) have brought few successes. Let us cast Truman's proposal into the numbers of the present. Should we now commit some 230 million Americans to the rescue of some 2500 million people elsewhere from the natural consequences of their having transgressed the carrying capacity of their environments? To effect this rescue by ourselves would mean that each American man, woman, and child would have to banish poverty for 10 other people, people of strikingly different cultures, ideals, and ways of looking at things—all this in a world of diminishing resources.

It is not going too far to say that the language of Point Four is an expression of moral imperialism, an ideal that continues to motivate many of our "best people." When Robert Kennedy announced that he was a candidate for President in 1968 he did so in these words: "At stake is not simply the leadership of our party, and even our own country, it is our right to the moral leadership of this planet" (44). The Greeks had a word for this attitude: *hubris,* arrogance. The Greeks also said, "Whom the gods would destroy they first make mad."

Yet we would like to help other people if we could. How might we help? The goods of this world come in only three modalities: substance, energy, and information. Any distribution of substance or energy by the system of the commons cannot be defended because, if continued, it leads to tragedy. Traffic in substance and energy is a zero-sum game: my gain is your loss, and vice versa. Not so with information, which does not obey conservation laws. Shared information can breed more information. We can afford to be completely generous with information, and I think we should be.

We should not, however, be under the illusion that any particular item of information given to another country will necessarily help it; used uncritically it may harm. Our best information is often no more than our best opinion, based on incomplete knowledge and treacherous theory. Although we have a hard time admitting this at any particular moment, we can recognize some of the errors we have made in the past.

There are fashions in foreign intervention as in other activities. Our advice to poor countries in the 1950s was *Industrialize!* When we realized the enormity of the need for capital formation we changed the tune: in the 60s we said *Mechanize!*, i.e., mechanize agriculture. Then came the "oil crisis" of 1973 and we changed our tune again: *Appropriatize!*, i.e., adopt the appropriate technology philosophy of Schumacher's *Small is Beautiful* (45). Is this the final word? Who knows? Some would have it that the common imperative running through all these attempts is *Develop!* But Edward Goldsmith has argued persuasively that the proper goal now is one of dedevelopment (46).

I suggest that we would show more respect for human dignity if we said something like the following to any people suffering from a longage of population. "We don't know the answers to your problems, but let us share with you all the little pieces of information we possess. Pick and choose from among the many ideas. Be prepared to learn from your mistakes: we have found no better policy for ourselves."

To minimize the pain of learning, three strategies can be recommended. First, learn from history (insofar as the lessons of history are relevant), and from the observation of other cultures. Second, whenever possible test a proposed change on a pilot plant scale. Third, augment experience with the prosthesis of theory. We don't have to jump off each new skyscraper to see if the descent is lethal: we can use the prosthetic structure of physical theory ($s = 1/2\ gt^2$, and all that) to give us an answer on which policy can confidently be built. Once in possession of a sound theory we can learn a good deal from purely intellectual trials with a minimum of suffering and waste. The most pressing problem for the social sciences is to create credible theory: without it, the human species will continue to suffer on a heroic scale.

The only sensible policy for international relations is to assert that national sovereignty (which every nation claims) mandates national responsibility (which most nations, like most people, will evade if they can). Demanding responsibility of others is *not* isolationism. Peaceful nations that trade with each other on a *quid pro quo* basis are involved in the sort of responsible relationship biologists call mutualism. It is parasitism when a nation refuses the discipline of *quid pro quo* trading and expects to be supported by gifts—euphemistically called "transfers" or "concessionary" rates of interest on "loans." The worst characteristic of parasitism is that it is addictive. A nation freed of the necessity of taking care of itself has little motivation to put an end to the growth of its population, and of the need that follows therefrom.

In real life all good policies must be compromised somewhat. Although in principle every nation should take care of itself, exceptions can sometimes be safely made, e.g., in the case of an earthquake. We can usefully distinguish between a crisis and a crunch (47). A crisis is a need that develops suddenly and can be alleviated in a short time by outside help, leaving the community essentially no worse off than it was before. An earthquake creates a crisis, because people don't intend to make a habit of having earthquakes. A crunch, on the other hand, is a persistent need arising out of overpopulation: alleviating the need creates more need. Bangladesh is caught in a crunch. Jan Narveson (48) has expressed well the difficult political issue posed by a crunch:

> 'We'll give you food, but on condition that you restrict your population growth to the point where the problem will eventually disappear instead of mushrooming to proportions which nobody can handle.' This type of condition, where it is relevant, seems to me reasonable. It is not reasonable to have a morality which makes it a duty to do self-defeating acts. And if your feeding me now means that in twenty years there will be five more in the same circumstances, then your aid *has* been self-defeating. (The political objections which have been made against insistence on reasonable programs of birth control impress me, thus far, as despicable hypocrisy.)

A few more words are in order about political objections. We should not be deterred by loud complaints voiced by members of a nation that we propose to deal with only on a *quid pro quo* basis. "Nation" is an abstraction. It is wrong to say that "Nation A objects." Nation A has no voice; only its citizens have voices. Only some of these voices are heard in the world outside.

Who are the people who set themselves up as spokesmen for poor nations? What gifts do they demand? And what will they do with the gifts if we accede to their demands? For a blatant example of how the power element of a demanding country sometimes behaves, consider this account of an event in Gabon, a West African nation of less than 600,000 people. The occasion was a reception for the Organization of African Unity given by President El Hadji Omar Bongo in July, 1977. The words are Daniel Patrick Moynihan's (49).

> President Bongo prepared a truly gala affair for his fellow leaders. He had built a reception hall in Libreville for some $250 million, including 52 villas for the delegation heads, two swimming pools, a luxurious night club, a sauna, a gymnasium, and two theatres. The complex had a unique feature: a viewing room between the two theatres which had a rotating floor, so that President Bongo could watch either stage by pushing a button. He did not have to go to the inconvenience of swiveling his chair. According to the *New York Times* account, the delegates to the conference were escorted from the airport by phalanxes of motorcycle outriders in frock coats (the delegates themselves rode in armored Cadillacs), and the parade route passed by guards in plumed kepis and crimson robes, as well as troups of singing and dancing women wearing T-shirts with President Bongo's picture on them.
>
> Now the nation of Gabon is quite wealthy. It has oil and other resources, and a per-capital income probably higher than that of the United States two generations ago. Yet its national debt is $1 billion, and the yearly interest on it is 23 percent of its annual budget.

This is no doubt an extreme case of parasitic prodigality, but we must never forget that donor generosity encourages the likes of Bongo. Whenever we yield to the demands of self-appointed spokesmen for poor countries we strengthen these people politically on their own turf. But when we refuse to meet the demands, the demanders lose in local power, and they *may*—we can assert no more—be replaced by other (and more responsible) spokesmen.

To some, the foregoing words will seem no more than the callous theorizing of a comfortable member of a rich country. I assure you this is not so. Many leaders in poor countries are intelligent enough to take an objective view of their true situation. We demean the citizens of other nations when we assume they must always be treated as children. Let us beware of the "white man's burden" under whatever rhetoric. Mao Tse-Tung, as long ago as 1945, proclaimed that the policy of the new China would be one of *tse li kong sheng*—"regeneration through our own efforts" (50). Foreign aid was rejected: national responsibility was asserted. China, then one of the poorest of the large countries of the world, stuck to this policy and did very well. Would she have done better had she adopted a parasitic mode of existence? Whey then do we encourage other poor countries to embrace parasitism? Is that the best that "compassion" can do?

In closing I return to Tinbergen's second argument, that we should *give* things to poor countries before they *take* them from us. How might they take, and what are the defenses against taking?

First, consider the possibility of war. Two centuries ago, in *The Wealth of Nations* (51), Adam Smith had this to say:

> In modern war the great expense of firearms gives an evident advantage to the nation which can best afford that expense, and consequently to an opulant and civilized over a poor and barbarous nation. In ancient times the opulant and civilized found it difficult to defend themselves against the poor and barbarous nations. In modern times the poor and barbarous find it difficult to defend themselves against the opulant and civilized.

Has the continued development of military technology since 1776 refuted this argument? It has not: the "Yom Kippur War" of 1973, ostensibly between Israel and the Arabs but truly financed and supplied by the U.S. and the U.S.S.R., lasted only 18 days but it went a long way toward bankrupting its financial backers. If opulant powers cannot finance a modern war, by what magic can the poor do so? By guerrilla actions a poor country can do very well protecting itself against invasion; but guerrilleros cannot themselves successfully invade other lands—which is the issue here.

Of course there is the nuclear bomb, which is now, alas! cheap; however, the missiles required to deliver it are of high technology and expensive. Nevertheless, it is conceivable that a poor country might, by considerable sacrifice, lob a few nuclear missiles over on us. Is it likely? I think not, for this reason. Such a venture could not be financed without the consent of the wealthy and powerful in the poor country. Before they would do that the wealthy would ask themselves what they had to gain by such an adventure. They would conclude: *Nothing*. They would see that the prudent course for them is to use their wealth to continue to keep their own threatening poor at bay. The idealistic among us may be repelled by this attitude, but I don't think we can find a really poor country in which the wealthy will sacrifice the well being of their families (the greatest reality to them) for a possible advantage to their nation (which, fortunately for us, they see as a secondary fiction).

However, there is the matter of terrorism and sabotage. That this is a major threat from now on there is no doubt. The faint of heart are always inclined to think they can buy off terrorists by yielding to their demands to redistribute the wealth. If we know anything at all about human nature it is this: yielding to terrorism always fails. Demands escalate. The demands would not even cease when a completely equitable distribution was achieved, because then there would be demands for compensation for the past. Meeting these demands would create a new inequity, and the bloody game would continue with a reversal of roles. *The only rational response to terrorism is police action:* it is not perfect but it is the best there is. Survival is impossible without police action in times of crisis, and the tacit threat of it at all times. This is the price we pay for civilization.

Now we must take up the third threat, that of forcible redistribution through aggressive, "peaceful," illegal immigration. Tinbergen, in a continuation of the passage quoted earlier, says that this mode of taking "has started already; there are today seven million illegal Mexican workers in the U.S." (Other authorities would put the number at more than 10 million.)

This, I think is the most telling point Tinbergen has to make. The process of takeover by uninvited guests has indeed started, and there is little sign—yet—that Americans are going to resist. Technically, it is easy to control immigration; politically it is not so easy. All too many of the rich suffer from a moral ambivalence, which has been vividly described in Raspail's chilling novel, *The Camp of the Saints* (52). Will America, like invaded France in Raspail's novel, continue to be immobilized by ambivalence in the face of a silent invasion? If we cannot muster the will to protect ourselves we will find that we have shared not wealth, but poverty with our invaders (53, 54). This fate, if it comes, will not be peculiarly American; it is the fate that awaits any nation that refuses to take the tragedy of the commons seriously.

REFERENCES

1. Tinbergen, J. 1978. Redistributing the world's wealth. Dev. Forum 6(3):3.
2. Aristotle. Politics, Book II, Chapter 3.
3. Hardin, G. 1968. The tragedy of the commons. Science 162:1243–1248.
4. Hardin, G. 1977. The Limits of Altruism, Chpt. 2. Indiana University Press, Bloomington, Ind.
5. Bullock, K., and Baden, J. 1977. Communes and the logic of the commons. In: G. Hardin and J. Baden (eds.), Managing the Commons. W. H. Freeman & Company, San Francisco.
6. Hardin, G. 1977. The Limits of Altruism, p. 30. Indiana University Press, Bloomington, Ind.

7. Hardin, G., and Baden, J. (eds.). 1977. Managing the Commons, Part III. W. H. Freeman & Company, San Francisco.

8. Marx, K. 1875. Critique of the Gotha program. In: R. C. Tucker (ed.). 1972. The Marx-Engels Reader. W. W. Norton & Company, New York.

9. Foxall, G. R. 1978. Agricultural improvement of common land: The relevance of co-operative management. J. Envir. Management 6:1–11.

10. Neustadtl, S. J. 1977. Montology: The ecology of mountains. Technol. Rev. 79(8):64.

11. Schultze, C. L. 1977. The Public Use of Private Interest. Brookings Institution, Washington, D.C.

12. Hardin, G. 1977. Will Xerox kill Gutenberg? Science 198:883. See also the follow-up letters in Science 199:122–125 (1978).

13. Hardin, G. 1974. Living on a lifeboat. BioScience 24:561–568.

14. Snow, C. P. 1955. The Two Cultures and the Scientific Revolution, p. 4. Cambridge University Press, Cambridge, England.

15. Carson, R. 1962. Silent Spring. Houghton Mifflin Company, Boston.

16. Farvar, M. T., and Milton, J. P. (eds.). 1972. The Careless Technology. Natural History Press, Garden City, N.Y.

17. Hardin, G. 1963. The cybernetics of competition. Persp. Biol. Med. 7:58–84. See section X. I believe this is the first publication of this aphorism, which Fortune magazine (February 1974, page 56) gratifyingly christened "Hardin's Law." (This article has been reprinted in reference 18.)

18. Hardin, G. 1978. Stalking the Wild Taboo, 2nd Ed. William Kaufmann, Los Altos, Cal.

19. George, C. J. 1972. The role of the Aswan Dam in changing the fisheries of the southwestern Mediterranean. In: M. T. Farvar and J. P. Milton (eds.), The Careless Technology. Natural History Press, Garden City, N.Y.

20. Popper, K. 1945. The Open Society and Its Enemies. Routledge & Kegan Paul, London.

21. Gabor, D. 1963. Inventing the Future, p. 18. Secker & Warburg, London.

22. Hardin, G. 1975. Will humanity learn from Nature? Sierra Club Bull. 60(8):41–43.

23. Wittgenstein, L. 1953. Philosophical Investigations, p. 47. Blackwell, Oxford.

24. Parkinson, C. N. 1957. Parkinson's Law, and Other Studies in Administration. Houghton Mifflin Company, Boston.

25. Hardin, G. 1977. Beyond 1776: Can Americans be well nourished in a starving world? Ann. N.Y. Acad. Sci. 300:87–91.

26. Klein, D. R. 1968. The introduction, increase, and crash of reindeer on St. Matthew Island. J. Wildlife Management 32:350–367.

27. Fremlin, J. H. 1964. How many people can the world support? New Sci. No. 415:285–287. (Reprinted in reference 28.)

28. Hardin, G. (ed.). 1969. Population, Evolution and Birth Control, 2nd Ed. W. H. Freeman & Company, San Francisco.

29. Christian Science Monitor, 28 June, 1978, page 1.

30. Schoeck, H. 1969. Envy. Harcourt Brace Jovanovich, Inc., New York.

31. Hardin, G. 1978. "Carrying Capacity." In: G. Hardin, Stalking the Wild Taboo, p. 260. William Kaufman, Los Altos, Cal.

32. Eckholm, E. 1976. Losing Ground. W. W. Norton & Company, New York.

33. Adelman, I., and Morris, C. 1973. Economic Growth and Social Equity in Developing Countries. Stanford University Press, Stanford.
34. Bauer, P. T. 1976. Dissent on Development, Rev. Ed. Harvard University Press, Cambridge, Mass.
35. Culbertson, J. M. 1971. Economic Development: An Ecological Approach. Alfred A. Knopf, Inc., New York.
36. Hamilton, W. B. (ed.). 1964. The Transfer of Institutions. Duke University Press, Durham, N.C.
37. Packenham, R. A. 1973. Liberal America and the Third World. Princeton University Press, Princeton, N. J.
38. Paddock, W., and Paddock, E. 1973. We Don't Know How. Iowa State University Press, Ames, Iowa.
39. Mamdani, M. 1973. The Myth of Population Control. Monthly Review Press, New York.
40. Molière, J. B. 1673. Le Malade Imaginaire, Act III, Scene 3.
41. Tuveson, E. L. 1968. Redeemer Nation, p. 125. University of Chicago Press, Chicago.
42. Phillips, C. 1966. The Truman Presidency, pp. 272–275. Macmillan Publishing Company, Inc., New York.
43. Galbraith, J. K. 1961. A positive approach to economic aid. Foreign Affairs 39:444–457.
44. Halberstam, D. 1969. The Best and the Brightest, p. 54. Fawcett, Greenwich, Conn.
45. Schumacher, E. F. 1973. Small is Beautiful. Harper & Row, New York.
46. Goldsmith, E. 1977. Dedeveloping the Third World. The Ecologist 7:338–339.
47. Hardin, G. 1976. Carrying capacity as an ethical concept. Soundings 59:120–137. (Reprinted in reference 18).
48. Aiken, W., and La Follette, H. (eds.). 1977. World Hunger and Moral Obligation, p. 64. Prentice-Hall, Inc., Englewood Cliffs, N.J.
49. Ledeen, M. A. 1978. Daniel Patrick Moynihan: The American political elite. Washington Rev. 1:34–41.
50. Berger, R. 1970. Self-reliance, past and present. Dev. Forum 6(3):3.
51. Smith, A. 1776. The Wealth of Nations, p. 669. Modern Library, 1937, New York.
52. Raspail, J. 1973. Le Camp des Saints. Translation by N. Shapiro (1975). Charles Scribners Sons, New York.
53. Hardin, G. 1977. Population and immigration: Compassion or responsibility? The Ecologist 7:268–272.
54. Hardin, G. 1978. The limits of sharing. World Issues Feb./Mar., pp. 5–10.

chapter 5

Justice, Freedom, and Sustainablity

Ian G. Barbour

Resource policies inescapably involve ethical as well as scientific issues. I consider these decisions in terms of three criteria: justice, freedom, and sustainability. Then I ask about the contributions of the biblical perspective to resource stewardship.

RESOURCE ETHICS

Resource Sustainability

First, we need to ask about the overall prospects for resource sustainability. What are the environmental constraints concerning food, energy, minerals, and other resources? What is the carrying capacity of the earth? If we turn to the experts, we will get rather divergent answers.

The Club of Rome study, directed by Dennis Meadows, was entitled *Limits to Growth* (1). It concludes that, unless industrial growth as well as population growth is halted within a few decades, we can expect worldwide catastrophe from resource depletion and environmental degradation. But the Hudson Institute study, *The Next 200 Years,* by Herman Kahn and others (2), anticipates ''a huge surplus of land, energy and resources,'' even if world population and per capita income each grow to four times their present levels. Kahn concludes that ''the resources of the earth will be more than sufficient—with a wide margin of safety—to sustain for an indefinite period of time and at high living standards the levels of population and economic growth we project.'' On this spectrum from pessimism to optimism, Dr. Hardin is as pessimistic as Meadows. Dr. Commoner and Dr. Obeng both seem to be somewhat on the optimistic side of the middle; neither of them is worried about the population problem, and both of them think that the right kinds of technology, and a more equitable distribution, can alleviate resource scarcities. I am not sure where Dr. Koopmans would place himself, since his analysis is more theoretical. Economists and engineers tend to be optimistic about resources, though few would go as far as Kahn.

How can experts disagree? The divergence arises in part from differing assumptions. Take, for example, the assumptions about technology. Kahn assumes that technological advances will continue to raise the efficiency of resource extraction and pollution control in the future, as they have in the past. He is confident that new technologies will make abundant energy available; this would be essential for his projections, since most of the other technologies on which he is counting are energy intensive. The pollution control technologies will add to production costs, he says, but we will be able to afford them in a growing economy. But Meadows assumes that technology is unlikely to achieve more than a fourfold improvement in efficiency without excessive environmental costs and a drain on capital needed in other sectors of the economy.

The divergence between optimists and pessimists arises also from the use of differing models. Kahn relies heavily on the economic model in which market mechanisms provide an automatic adjustment to resource scarcities. When a resource becomes scarce, its price will rise, which will cut down on resource use. The price rise will also increase the supply by encouraging the search for new reserves, better extraction techniques, and substitute materials and processes. At the other extreme, Meadows, like Hardin, relies on the environmental model, which starts from a finite carrying capacity and resource base. Market mechanisms can stimulate new technologies to extend the carrying capacity somewhat, but rapidly diminishing returns and increasing environmental costs are encountered.

Now, every model is selective. A model portrays the features of the world and the kinds of causal relationships that you think are most important in predicting the future. But every model leaves out a lot, and therefore has its limitations. The economic model is most useful in predicting short term adjustments in a relatively free market when supply and demand are strongly price dependent. But because it discounts the future, as Dr. Koopmans pointed out, the market gives little weight to the needs of future generations. It neglects environmental costs, except where these are internalized through legislated standards or taxes. In extreme scarcity, when there are no substitutes, market mechanisms break down. The environmental model, by contrast, is most relevant in considering long time horizons, or in dealing in the short run with fragile ecosystems, but it tends to neglect the possibilities for creative human responses that could reduce the environmental impact of our resource use.

I believe we must take the long view, but I will suggest that the right kinds of technology can make a substantial contribution in extending resource limits. A doubling of world food production in a generation is by no means impossible, but a tripling would severely strain environmental, where Dr. Koopmans would place himself, since his analysis is more theoretical. Economists and engineers tend to be optimistic about resources, though few would go as far as Kahn.

energy, and land constraints (3, 4). I am more hopeful than Hardin about the expansion of the earth's carrying capacity, although I agree that the wrong technologies could rapidly erode it. The constraints that we now face are social and political as much as physical or environmental. If population levels off at 10 billion, there are enough resources for all if they are wisely used and equitably distributed. I would reject both a no-growth pessimism and a pro-growth optimism; our goal should be selective and sustainable growth. The key questions are: Whose growth? What kind of growth? Neither the economic model nor the environmental model says anything about the distribution of resources among individuals or groups, which I believe is the crucial issue today. We have to draw from politics and ethics in addition to ecology, economics, and technology (5, 6).

Distributive Justice

Let me turn to the question of distributive justice, and at the same time respond more directly to Dr. Hardin. I would want first to express gratitude for his writings over the years. His 1968 essay, "The Tragedy of the Commons," which has been reprinted in some fifty anthologies, is a powerful statement of the interconnection of population growth and environmental destruction. I agree with most of the first half of his address today, in which he talks about the commons and ecological interdependence. But the further he gets from animal populations, the more dubious I am. I want to raise five issues about the relation between rich and poor nations.

1. Inequalities in resource use. Hardin mentions that each person in a rich country consumes from 20 to 40 times as much resources as a person in a poor country. But he says that if the rich nations reduced their resource use, it wouldn't help the poor nations. Wealth cannot be shared, he says; only poverty can be shared. It seems to me that this ignores the way our resource use affects the carrying capacity of other nations. Take the case of energy, which each of us uses at 100 times the rate of the poorest quarter of mankind (7). Our huge oil imports contribute to the high price of the oil that is desperately needed by third world countries for fertilizer and irrigation pumps. Oil that we burn will be forever unavailable to developing nations or future generations. This is an issue of justice between nations and between generations.

Consider the consumption of food. In some Central American countries where half the children are malnourished, more than half the agricultural land is used for export crops. In many parts of the world, the legacy of colonialism is perpetuated in the use of scarce land for nonfood crops such as coffee and tea. Our luxuries reduce the carrying capacity of other countries. The global food problem is in part a question of maldistribution. Current food production would provide more than twice the minimum calorie and protein requirements for every man, woman, and child alive today if it were uniformly distributed (8). Our meat consumption is particularly wasteful. Only 4% of the protein content of the grain consumed by cattle ever appears on the table as meat. Ninety percent of the world protein deficit could be met by the grain and fish meal fed to U.S. cattle alone (9, 10). But of course the key question is not the distribution of existing food, which would involve huge transportation problems, but rather the overall increase and better distribution of food prodution capacity.

2. Foreign aid.   Hardin says that aid creates dependency and parasitism, and that the alleviation of persistent needs only leads to more need. I submit that some forms of aid do create dependency, but other forms lead to greater self-reliance. Certainly, emergency food aid does nothing to cure the causes of hunger; taken alone, it might indeed encourage dependency. But assistance in agricultural development can increase the productivity, the carrying capacity, and the self-reliance of other nations. In the 1960s most development assistance was aimed at economic growth and industrialization, mainly on the western model of capital-intensive industry. Often a privileged minority benefited enormously while poverty and unemployment for the majority increased.

But during the 1970s, development experts have been advocating a new approach, a strategy oriented toward basic human needs. The leaders of the World Bank have said that the distribution of benefits is as important as aggregate economic growth. Since 1975, U.S. foreign aid, although very inadequate, has been aimed at rural development and basic needs. New development strategies call for wider access to land, credit, and education to increase the productivity of the small farmer and the landless peasant. Labor-intensive rather than capital-intensive technologies are sought, so that employment will increase (11, 12). Some aid projects, such as the Aswan Dam, did indeed have serious environmental consequences. Yet the lesson, surely, is not that all development assistance is harmful, but that indirect impacts should be analyzed in advance, especially for large scale projects. In many cases there may be more appropriate small scale technologies. For example, technical assistance in designing cheap solar cookers would have far-reaching benefits throughout the Third World in halting deforestation from the use of wood for cooking, and such assistance would not be "an immense diversion of capital," but a relatively modest expenditure. Each of us pays $450 annually in taxes for defense but only $6 for development aid (13). If this figure were doubled and wisely allocated it could contribute significantly, with very little sacrifice on our part.

3. Population control.   I am in complete agreement about the importance of lowered birth rates, but I believe this can be achieved most rapidly by a combination of family planning programs and social and economic development. The nations in which major reductions in birth rates have occurred are all countries in which the benefits of development have been widely distributed among the population. The list includes countries with political systems as varied as China and Taiwan, South Korea and Costa Rica, Sri Lanka and Malaysia. These nations all have family planning programs, but, equally important, they all offer wide access to education and health care. Greater economic security, later marriages, and gains in the status of women have also contributed (14, 15).

A prime example is Kerala, the only state in India in which fertility has fallen sharply. It is one of the poorest states, but it has a history of land reforms and educational reforms. Both the literacy rate and the life expectancy are far above other Indian states because basic education and health care are widely available. Compared to Kerala, many Latin American countries have 10 times the per capita GNP, but income and social services are very unevenly distributed, and birth rates have remained high. I suggest that distributive justice within nations is relevant to population policy as well as to resource policy (16).

4. The global commons.   Hardin says that freedom in an unmanaged commons brings ruin to all. "Either the commons must be broken up or it must be managed." He himself chooses the first alternative, that of breaking up the commons by emphasizing national boundaries. I would choose the second, international management of the global commons, because I don't think we can break them up. The ecological lesson of interdependence applies to nations as well as species. We share the oceans and the air, and we need each other's natural resources. It would seem to me sheer hypocrisy to cut off our miniscule foreign aid in the name of avoiding intervention overseas, while our multinational corporations continue to intervene on a massive scale. The profit on overseas investment by U.S. corporations averages twice their rate of return on domestic investment. It is the multinational corporations, more than foreign aid, that tend to strengthen ruling elites, transfer inappropriate technologies, and in some cases support repressive regimes opposed to political reforms.

Hardin evidently sees international trade as a way of combining interdependence and privatism (the breaking up of the commons). But if some very powerful nations set the terms of trade, they can exploit other nations and treat the world as a commons again. Rich nations, for example, control most of the transportation and processing of raw materials. They talk about free trade but in practice they put up protective tariffs against manufactured goods, which tends to keep developing countries in their role as suppliers of raw materials. So I would side with Tinbergen in advocating steps toward the international management of the global commons, steps toward cooperation rather than confrontation. This would involve strengthening the United Nations, as I suggest shortly.

  5. The vulnerability of industrial nations.   Hardin sees no real danger from nuclear terrorism or other desperate actions by resentful and frustrated nations. I agree that the ruling elites are unlikely to launch a nuclear war, but in a world of nuclear proliferation, especially if plutonium is in wide use, it would be relatively easy for revolutionary groups to make nuclear explosives with which to blackmail affluent nations. Hijacking, bombing, and the sabotage of nuclear plants would be hard to prevent, even if we greatly extended police powers. I also suggest that oil prices, inflation, and the falling dollar have underscored our economic vulnerability and our interdependence.

Freedom and Coercion

Let me turn now from issues of justice to issues of freedom in a world of resource scarcities. A number of authors have said that increasingly coercive measures will be needed to deal effectively with impending crises. For example, William Ophuls' book, *Ecology and the Politics of Scarcity* (17) argues that democracy is doomed. In crises, people accept authoritarian governments with powers to compel obedience. Moreover, when there are dangers which people do not understand, they accept decisions by competent experts. In the name of survival, says Ophuls, we will have to accept drastic restrictions of personal liberty. Faced with catastrophe, the sacrifice of freedom is the lesser evil.

  An even gloomier prospect is offered by Robert Heilbroner (18). He starts with a grim picture of population growth, widespread starvation, and environmental deterioration. Only authoritarian regimes could organize society to face such catastrophes. Democratic institutions will be unable to cope with internal strife, international conflict, and threats to survival. Dissent and freedom of expression will be looked on as the obsolete luxury of self-indulgent intellectuals. Heilbroner anticipates massive crop failures, social breakdown, and wars of redistribution; only after convulsive social change and the disintegration of industrial civilization might a more primitive society emerge from the ruins.

I have indicated that I do not share the pessimism of these authors concerning resource limits, but I also see more hope of peaceful change through democratic processes. Granted, the individualistic view of freedom typical of the American frontier is no longer tenable. Freedom understood as the absence of governmental interference is indeed obsolete in an interdependent world. However, freedom understood as participation in the decisions that affect one's life is still important and remains the only defense against the abuse of power. Authoritarian leaders might initially act in the common good, but there is ample historic precedent for expecting that they would become a new ruling elite protecting their own interests. Coercion is indeed needed, but it can be introduced democratically and its harsher forms can be avoided. Economic incentives and strong regulations with legal sanctions can alter behavior patterns without undermining civil liberties or creating a totalitarian society.

There are two major obstacles to effective resource legislation. One is the reluctance of the public to take resource scarcities seriously or to accept sacrifices for the sake of conservation. The other is the alliance of political leaders with particular economic interests. All too often a powerful alliance forms between a congressional committee, a federal agency, and an industry—for example, the triangle between the Armed Services Committees, the Department of Defense, and the defense contractors, or that between the Joint Committee on Atomic Energy, the Atomic Energy Commission, and the nuclear industry, which for so long promoted nuclear energy. But, if enough people are concerned, it is possible to get around these power structures, as happened in the early seventies when Congress defeated the supersonic transport (SST) and the antiballistic missile (ABM). There are also opportunities through the courts for citizens and public interest groups to challenge the actions of federal agencies or industries, as environmentalists have effectively done in a number of cases.

However, large scale technologies are becoming increasingly difficult to control through democratic processes. They are so capital intensive that they can be developed only by giant corporations and government bureaucracies. They lead to a further concentration of economic power, and therefore also of political power, among those who are already powerful. Sophisticated systems such as nuclear plants are difficult for the public to understand; critical decisions are made by technical experts with minimal public participation. Moreover, complex large scale systems often turn out to have indirect effects that even the experts did not anticipate. They are likely to be vulnerable to human error and to deliberate sabotage by disaffected groups. Because of the risks of large scale disaster, they may have to be subjected to elaborate security measures. Centralized technologies, in short, encourage economic and political centralization (19).

There are some technical systems that by their nature have to be centrally controlled, such as long distance communication and transportation. There are others, such as steel production, in which centralized plants are justified because economies of scale are so great they outweigh other considerations. However, in many cases apparent economies of scale reflect direct or indirect subsidies, or the neglect of environmental and social costs. By contrast, decentralized, intermediate scale technologies are usually labor intensive rather than capital intensive, and therefore provide more jobs. They strengthen rural areas rather than contributing to urban migration. Appropriate technologies can be designed to use local materials and to be responsive to local needs. They are not necessarily environmentally benign, but they at least avoid the large scale dangers and the concentrated environmental assaults typical of centralized technologies. Above all, decentralization offers opportunities for citizen participation and local control in the interest of freedom. Later I consider solar energy as an illustration of some of these advantages.

RESOURCE STEWARDSHIP

Individual Life-styles

I turn now to some examples of resource stewardship in relation to justice, freedom, and sustainability. I start with individual life-styles. The dominant American ideal is a high consumption life-style. Twenty-five billion dollars are spent in the U.S. each year on advertising, which comes to $115 per person—more than the annual income of a quarter of humankind. Advertising stimulates demand for all kinds of new commodities. A barrage of TV commercials tells us that deodorants, cigarettes, soft drinks, and breakfast cereals are vital to our well being. The mass media hold before us the images of success of an acquisitive culture. In a consumer society, personal identity is defined by possessions, and fulfillment is equated with rising levels of consumption.

William Leiss (20) has argued that our society encourages people to seek the satisfaction of all their diverse needs through consumption. We know, of course, that overeating is often an attempt to use food as a substitute for self-acceptance and acceptance by others. Similarly, we use commodities to satisfy needs for status and happiness that could better be fulfilled in less resource-consumptive ways. Leiss urges us to move toward nonconsumptive sources of satisfaction, such as creative activity, human relationships, and shared decision making. U.S. consumption patterns, he says, are not only excessive relative to the basic needs of other people; they also reflect a misinterpretation of our own genuine fulfillment. Both poverty and affluence seem to be inimical to human fulfillment. Once our basic needs are met we should be free to concentrate on other levels of self-realization and community life.

There are thus multiple motives for simpler life-styles. Reduced consumption can be motivated by sustainability, since it reduces resource depletion and pollution. It can be motivated by social justice if it is an act of solidarity with the world's poor, an acknowledgment of past and present injustices in the relationships between nations. In other words, it can express a personal commitment to a more equitable distribution of resources. Again, a simpler life-style can be an assertion of freedom in taking greater control of your own life and refusing to be manipulated by the overt and hidden persuaders of a consumer society. A simpler life-style reflects an alternative vision of human fulfillment, a redefinition of the good life. You can give priority to persons rather than things, to cooperation rather than competition, to significant work rather than mere wage earning. Resource use is always part of a whole pattern of living.

What can one person do in the face of the global problems we have been talking about? Each of us can begin with his or her own life. Here are some samples.

1. Resource conservation.   Energy conservation is a matter of individual action as well as national policy. We can use smaller cars, bicycles, or public transportation. Home energy use can be reduced by insulation, solar heating, and eliminating air conditioning. Appliances can be judged by their energy consumption and their life-cycle costs (which allow for durability and operating costs as well as initial cost). A household can cut down resource waste, such as throw-away containers and excessive packaging, and can recycle waste paper, glass, and aluminum. These are modest measures that entail no great sacrifices. A more radical reduction in consumption would involve getting along with fewer consumer products and fewer household appliances—or perhaps sharing equipment with others in communal living situations such as extended families, cooperative houses, or urban or rural communes (21).

2. Food for health—and for justice.   Seventy million Americans are overweight. It is ironic that we suffer from diseases caused by overeating, like heart disease, while other countries have diseases from malnutrition. For the sake of health, we should reduce our food consumption, particularly of fats and sugars. We should eat more natural foods in place of the overprocessed, overpackaged, artificially flavored products that fill the supermarkets. For the sake of justice, we should reduce our use of such nonfood crops as coffee, tea, tobacco, and grains for alcohol, production of which ties up land needed for food—especially land in developing countries. Reducing meat consumption or adopting a vegetarian diet would save huge quantities of grain, as we have seen. Eating "lower on the food chain" can provide adequate nutrition with less waste.

3. Significant work.   In a consumer society, most people look on work only as a source of income to spend on consumption. Instead, a person can seek work that is meaningful in itself. This might involve production aimed at basic human needs, or human services that are not resource intensive. Industrial societies have sharply separated production from consumption and daily life, but there are a variety of ways of relating work to the life of the community in small scale workshops, producers' cooperatives, craft collectives, and communal farms. In such settings people can have greater control over their own lives and participate more directly in work-related decisions (22, 23).

4. Political involvement.   Individual life-styles and political action can be mutually reinforcing. Only public decisions can initiate public transportation. Reducing meat consumption conserves grain, but apart from new national policies it does not benefit the malnourished. Each person can by both word and deed influence people's attitudes and help to create new constituencies that can act through political processes. Political representatives do respond if enough citizens are concerned. Public apathy is the main obstacle to more effective legislation for conservation and the more equitable distribution of resources.

Energy Policy

My next example, energy policy, is at the level of national rather than individual action. I agree with Dr. Commoner about the advantages of solar energy, which gets high marks on each of my three criteria. It is *sustainable* indefinitely, since it draws from the sun itself. It is nonpolluting and safe. There is no way you can divert it to make weapons, and there are no risks to pass on to future generations, as there are with radioactive wastes. There is one major environmental impact, the use of land for solar-electric installations, but in most regions land could be used that is not useful for agriculture. Solar energy is flexible in scale. You can build large units if you need large blocks of electricity, but you can also build smaller dispersed units, which reduce the costs of transmission and distribution. Dr. Commoner dealt with the two main problems today, namely, energy storage and initial costs.

Solar energy also scores high on *justice*. Sunlight is rather evenly distributed among nations and regions, whereas oil, coal, and uranium are very unevenly distributed. Cheap solar technology would be a great boon to the sun-rich Third World. Nuclear reactors, by contrast, would be of limited use, since there are only a few areas that have the power grids to distribute huge blocks of electricity; developing countries would be dependent on industrial nations for nuclear expertise as well as fuel. Solar equipment is easier to understand, requires no fuel, and is labor intensive rather than capital intensive, so it would encourage self-reliance rather than dependency. Solar cookers, solar water pumps, biogas disgesters, and photovoltaic panels would be especially useful in the Third World (24, 25).

Solar energy can also contribute to *freedom*. Nuclear energy, and especially the breeder reactor, is the epitome of a centralized capital-intensive technology. The breeder would be even more expensive than current reactors and more vulnerable to accident, sabotage, terrorism, and the diversion of material for nuclear weapons. It would represent a further concentration of economic and political power, and would require more extensive regulation and tighter security measures. Solar energy, on the other hand, provides many opportunities for decentralization and local participation and control. It would encourage small-town industries and businesses, and local installation and repair shops. Community systems of intermediate scale, serving a few thousand homes, would permit the co-generation of electricity and heat and would offer scope for community participation (26).

So I agree with Commoner that solar energy is preferable to the breeder as a long term source, and I agree that we should put much greater effort into solar development. We have been incredibly shortsighted in heavily subsidizing nonrenewable fuels—first oil and then uranium—and we must tip the balance the other way now. But I do not agree with Commoner that we can rely on oil and natural gas for the transition. His estimates of recoverable oil and gas are much higher than most estimates (see, for example, reference 27). Also oil is needed by other countries, and by future generations, for fertilizer and petrochemicals as well as fuel. I believe that the U.S. will have to make considerable use of coal during the transition, and that some nations, such as Japan and Western Europe, which lack our vast coal reserves, may have to make use of nuclear power (although I hope they will avoid breeders and reprocessing plants that would make the diversion of plutonium for weapons much easier). But the use of coal could be kept down by an intensive program of energy conservation, which was not emphasized by Commoner.

Conservation clearly contributes to *sustainability*. It extends the time available to improve current technologies and to develop sounder alternatives. It reduces the huge waste of irreplaceable resources in our present practices, and it conserves supplies for future generations. Measures to save a given amount of energy have much less impact on environment and health than any known way of producing and consuming the same amount of energy, and in general conservation is cheaper than an equivalent increase in production. Several European countries have levels of income, health, and education similar to ours with 40% less energy consumption per capita (28).

What about *justice?* Conservation helps to reduce our grossly disproportionate energy use compared to developing nations, but what about justice within the U.S., and the inequitable impact of higher energy prices on low-income families? Here there seems to be a conflict between sustainability and justice. For example, most environmentalists favored the deregulation of natural gas, because an artificially low price has stimulated consumption. A higher price on fossil fuels would also reflect their greater environmental and social costs, and would encourage the shift to renewable sources. But in the name of justice, consumer groups opposed deregulation, which would hit poor families hardest. Dr. Commoner is dedicated to both environmentalism and justice, but in this case he sides with the consumer groups. I would submit that conservation and justice can be combined with the kind of policy President Carter initially proposed: higher gas prices and well-head oil taxes coupled with rebates to low-income families.

What about *freedom?* Should conservation be voluntary or mandatory? In the name of freedom, economists tend to rely on the marketplace, supplemented by tax incentives. There will be some energy saving by both industry and consumers as a voluntary response to higher energy prices, but effective conservation requires a larger role for government intervention through subsidies, mandatory standards (such as building insulation, auto mileage, and appliance efficiency), and the promotion of public transportation and less energy-intensive technologies. I believe we will need both higher prices and mandatory changes in public policy, as well as changes in attitudes, values, and life-styles, in order to realize zero energy growth.

The Global Compact

I have given some examples of resource ethics at the levels of individual action and national policy. The final example concerns the possibilities for global cooperation in resource stewardship. There are, of course, a number of agencies of the United Nations that take a global approach to resource problems—for example, the Food and Agriculture Organization, and the U.N. Environmental Program with which Dr. Obeng has been associated. These agencies are doing important work in gathering information, in fostering greater awareness, and in coordinating action among nations. But I want to discuss how the role of the U.N. in global resource allocation might be expanded even further.

Starting with the Sixth Special Session of the U.N. General Assembly in 1974, Third World nations have been calling for a New International Economic Order. Many of these nations achieved political independence after World War II, but faced continued economic dependence and the growing gap between rich and poor countries. Since 1974, spokesmen for the Third World have been asking not for charity but for a more just international order and greater control of their own destinies. Too often, they said, the rules of the international game have been stacked against them. The industrial nations talk about a free market, but they put up protective walls with tariffs and quotas against manufactured goods. Poor nations are thereby locked into their roles as suppliers of raw materials. Third World countries called for the abolition of tariffs, more favorable terms of trade, the encouragement of indigenous processing of raw materials, and the regulation of multinational corporations.

The first reaction of the industrial nations to these demands was outright rejection. They said that Third World nations were trying to blame all their problems on someone else without asking what they themselves could do. But today the initial rhetoric of confrontation has cooled off and there is more serious discussion and negotiation of specific issues. The progress to date has been limited, but there are voices on both sides speaking for global cooperation.

There have been several proposals that would tie together changes within developing nations, changes in industrial nations, and changes in the international order. One of these is the recent study for the Club of Rome, *Reshaping the International Order* (29), edited by Jan Tinbergen, to whom Dr. Hardin referred. The report advocates a global compact between rich and poor countries. The compact would be based partly on common interests, such as avoiding nuclear war and creating a stable international monetary system, but it would also be based on negotiated trade-offs of divergent interests. In such negotiation, the bargaining position of some developing countries is likely to improve. In many ways, OPEC is unique because so many nations are so heavily dependent on oil, but agreements among other raw material producers can be expected in the future. The U.S. now imports more than half its supplies of 20 critical industrial materials. We are vulnerable to world economic and political instability, especially if nuclear proliferation continues.

The global compact would require that the development strategies of poor nations be aimed at basic human needs. Their development plans would have to be approved, not by donor nations, but by a U.N. development agency. In some countries these plans might involve land reform, rural development, appropriate technology, and social programs including literacy, health, and family planning, to control population growth. The rich countries, for their part, would have to reduce resource waste and adopt policies of selective growth, stressing services rather than resource-intensive industries. By abolishing tariffs they would also encourage resource processing and manufacturing in the Third World.

The Tinbergen report advocates a strengthening and expansion of U.N. agencies to deal with food, technology, energy, and environmental protection. In place of unpredictable aid from donors to recipients, there would be a World Development Authority with its own independent sources of long term funding. Some of these funds would come from royalties or taxes on seabed mining, ocean fisheries, and other resources seen as the common heritage of mankind. Eventually a world tax on all mining of nonrenewable resources might be introduced. The report urges expansion of peace-keeping forces and institutions for conflict resolution, such as a world court operating under a system of international law. Arms control and disarmament are of course crucial to the funding of development as well as to world peace. Four hundred billion dollars is spent on arms each year; with even a fraction of this amount, basic human needs could be met around the world in a generation.

Such a strengthened U.N. would clearly contribute to sustainability and to justice. In particular, international taxation would be a crucial instrument of global *justice*. Within our nation, we recognize the need for distributive justice. We know that economic power is self-perpetuating, so that from market forces alone the gaps between rich and poor increase. We counteract this tendency by legislating progressive income taxes, unemployment compensation, social security, and minimum levels of education, food, and health care. We use political processes to correct major imbalances in the economic order. There are no comparable mechanisms at the international level to prevent the gaps between rich and poor from increasing. In the long run, only a more just world will be a stable world.

But wouldn't a stronger U.N. involve a centralization of authority that would diminish *freedom*? Some forms of freedom would indeed be restricted, but other forms would be enhanced. The overall structure would remain participatory. The developing nations would achieve greater self-determination and a more democratic voice in international decision making. The areas of global authority would be limited and functionally defined, in contrast to the unlimited powers of an all-embracing world government. Policy would be centrally coordinated, but administration would be as decentralized as possible. Many of the desired results would come from the design and automatic operation of policies like taxation that do not require continual central intervention. There should be deliberate provision for cultural diversity and for diverse regional emphases consistent with global sustainability and justice.

Is such a global future a utopian dream, an impractical ideal? Clearly such changes will not happen overnight. They depend on a new international outlook, a recognition of global interdependence, and an extension of loyalties beyond the national state. I discuss below how such global consciousness might be fostered.

RELIGIOUS PERSPECTIVES

The Biblical Tradition

I want to look now at the contribution that the biblical perspective might make to resource stewardship. Four themes are particularly relevant. In each case I start from the prophets of ancient Israel who, like us, lived in times of national crisis and international conflict.

1. Commitment to social justice. The prophets attacked the inequalities of their society because they believed in the fundamental equality of all persons before God. The oppression of the poor, they said, violates the demands of a God of justice. Hear the words of Amos:

> For three transgressions of Israel, and for four, I will not revoke the punishment; because they sell the righteous for silver, and the needy for a pair of shoes—they that trample the head of the poor into the dust of the earth, and turn aside the way of the afflicted. . . . But let justice roll down like waters, and righteousness like an ever-flowing stream (Amos 2:6, 5:24).

Jesus opened his ministry with a quotation from Isaiah. "The spirit of the Lord is upon me, because he has anointed me to preach good news to the poor. He has sent me to proclaim release to the captives and recovery of sight to the blind, to set at liberty those who are oppressed" (Luke 4:18). Admittedly, Jesus spoke more often about love than about justice—in part, perhaps, because he lived in an occupied country that no longer controlled its own national life. Love and justice are not identical, but they rest alike on the value of the person. Justice is often the form that love must take in dealing with groups and social structures.

Social justice has remained central in the Christian tradition, despite the very mixed record of the church as an institution. Religion has often been a conservative force with a vested interest in the status quo, but it has also been a major source of leadership in creative social movements, such as hospital and prison reform and the abolition of slavery in the 19th century, or the civil rights and anti-war movements of the 1960s. Recent statements from the Roman Catholic Church and the World Council of Churches have focused on global justice in resource policies. Here is one sentence from an address by biologist Charles Birch at a recent World Council assembly: "The rich must live more simply that the poor may simply live" (30). A more equitable distribution of resources, you see, is a demand of social justice, not just an act of individual charity.

2. Long term stewardship. The prophets used an extended time scale because they believed that God's purposes extend into the future. They spoke of obligations to a God who spans the generations. There are obligations to posterity; for example, the land is held as a trust for future generations. There is a solidarity in time, a covenant "from generation to generation." "The earth is the Lord's" and the whole creation is part of God's purpose. Because all forms of life are within his plan, we are accountable for the way we treat them. The fields are to lie fallow every seventh year; the land deserves respect and it will cry out if it is misused. A number of the psalms express a joyful appreciation for the world of nature.

Subsequent Christian thought has been very diverse. A one-sided emphasis on man's dominion over nature has often overshadowed the stewardship theme, as Lynn White has pointed out. But there were other voices. White himself nominates St. Francis as patron saint for the ecology movement because of his deep love for the natural world and sense of unity with it. I would agree with René Dubos that St. Benedict is a better model. St. Benedict combined a practical approach with respect for the earth and care of it. The Benedictine monasteries developed sound agricultural practices, such as crop rotation and soil conservation. They drained swamps and husbanded timber all over Europe. Better still, we can go back to the Bible itself to recover a sense of stewardship of nature. The idea of a created order provides an inclusive framework that encompasses all forms of life and all periods of time. Isn't that what sustainability is all about (31)?

3. A broad view of human fulfillment. For the prophets, the good life is identified not with material possessions, but with personal existence in community. They recognized the dangers of both poverty and affluence. They saw the harmful consequences of affluence for the rich as well as for the poor. Jesus in turn stressed the importance of feeding the hungry, but he also said that "man does not live by bread alone," and he vividly portrayed the dangers of wealth. The earliest Christian community, as described in Acts, "had all things in common." Distribution was made to each "as any had need." Over the ensuing centuries the monastic orders preserved the ideals of simplicity and community. The Reformation and particularly the Puritan movement upheld frugality and simplicity, and were critical of "the luxuries of the rich."

Today, in an overconsumptive society, we need not only this negative attack on materialism, but the positive witness to the priority of the personal and the quality of the life of a community. New life-styles arise not only from a concern for global justice, but also from a new vision of the good life, a focus on sources of satisfaction that are not resource consumptive. Here religious faith can speak to the crisis of meaning that underlies the pursuit of affluence. One example is the book, *Enough is Enough*, by the British theologian John Taylor, which urges restraint in consumption, a level of "material sufficiency" that is neither affluence nor poverty (32; see also 33). An American group has expressed in the Shakertown Pledge a religious commitment to such goals as creative simplicity, ecological soundness, occupational accountability, and global justice (34). I believe that the biblical vision of human fulfillment can strengthen the search for simpler lifestyles today.

4. Judgment and hope. To the crises of their day the prophets of ancient Israel brought a double message that has particular contemporary relevance. On the one hand, they spoke of God's judgment on the structures of human greed. They saw even military defeat and national catastrophe as forms of divine judgment on materialism, idolatry, and injustice. The prophets were realistic about human sinfulness and aware of the dangers when economic and political power are concentrated in the hands of any group or nation. Their first word was a call to repentance and humility. Today such humility might be an antidote to the Promethean pride to which industrial nations are prone. Obviously the prophets said nothing about technological centralization, but I suspect that if we accepted their view of human nature we would be hesitant to rely too heavily on large scale systems that are vulnerable to human frailty and the abuse of institutional power. Perhaps for us, too, catastrophe will be a form of judgment on an unrepentant nation.

But the other side of the prophetic message is hope. Beyond judgment and repentance there is reconciliation and redemption. Reconciliation is restoration of wholeness, the overcoming of alienation from God, from nature, and from other persons. Redemption is creative renewal in response to God's redemptive activity. The ultimate symbol of hope is the vision of a future Kingdom of peace and brotherhood. In Micah's words:

> They shall beat their swords into plowshares and their spears into pruning hooks; nation shall not lift up sword against nation, neither shall they learn war any more; but they shall sit every man under his vine and under his fig tree, and none shall make them afraid (Micah 4:3–4).

The prophetic imagination pictured a future harmony that would include all mankind and all nature. Every person would be at peace with his neighbor and with the created order. There is a tension between particularism and universalism in biblical religion, as in all religions, but in the final vision universalism is dominant. The image of the Kingdom gathers up the themes of justice, creation, and human fulfillment.

The idea of the Kingdom took many forms in subsequent history. Some members of the early church expected it to come very soon on earth. Others visualized the Kingdom as another world, a heavenly realm that is unrelated to this world. More commonly it has been understood both as the goal of history and as beyond history. The Lord's Prayer includes both aspects: "Thy Kingdom come, they will be come, on earth, as it is in heaven." The Kingdom is indeed an imaginative vision, but it is not just an idle dream. Like all visions of the future, it influences the way we interpret the present. It leads us to see the world in a new way. We see both judgment and renewal in history, and act in response to them. These biblical themes, I suggest, can contribute significantly to resource stewardship today.

Sources of Change

Finally, what sources of change might help us move toward resource stewardship in a just, free, and sustainable world? Let me list four of them.

First, *education* is a far-reaching instrument of social change. Education in the schools has begun to spread environmental awareness and a rudimentary global awareness, but it could do much more in both areas. However, the education of a new generation is a slow process, and teachers only gradually depart from what they themselves were taught. Adult education can be more rapid. Citizens' movements and voluntary community groups can provide information and help to raise the consciousness of the public. It was only seven years from Rachel Carson's *Silent Spring* to the National Environmental Policy Act. The churches also have a considerable potential for fostering responsible stewardship. Education for an age of resource scarcities must deal with both facts and values, information and attitudes, cognitive processes and affective responses.

Second, *crisis and disaster* can speed the process by challenging prevailing assumptions. Perhaps oil spills, gasoline shortages, electricity blackouts, and widespread famines will have to occur on a more massive scale before people will wake up. Taken alone, however, crises may lead to undesirable changes. Governments may rely on "technical fixes" whose indirect costs turn out to be high; when these fail the reaction may be pessimism and despair. But in combination with the vision of positive alternatives, crises can be catalysts for constructive action. In emergencies such as war or natural disaster, people will make sacrifices for the common good—provided that the sacrifices are shared, the common good is clear, and a more hopeful future is envisaged. There is hope if, along with resource crises, there is new respect for the earth, new dedication to justice and freedom, and new visions of the good life. There is hope of averting disaster—or of rebuilding a world beyond disaster if we do not act soon enough to avert it.

Third, *political power* can greatly accelerate processes of social change. Sometimes a coalition formed around common or overlapping interests can become a new force for political change within a nation. In the international arena, I have noted the new bargaining power that is being acquired by raw material producers, and by nations gaining access to nuclear weapons. Both domestic and international unrest in a world of scarcities and inflation will be potent sources of change, but, again, the changes may be destructive. Domestic pressures for reform could lead to reaction and repression. Pressures from abroad could lead the U.S. to isolationism and a fortress mentality. The limited gains from the civil rights movement of the 1960s would not have occurred without political pressures from the Black community, but without at least some national dedication to justice, Black power would probably have simply evoked further repression and violence. So, too, with global resources. Only a more inclusive vision can direct political power so that conflict becomes a step toward a just and peaceful world rather than a step away from it. We should not underestimate the strength of individual and institutional greed.

Fourth, *new visions* can provide the motivation and direction for creative social change. Moral exhortation seldom inspires action among those who are reluctant to change. Visions, on the other hand, present positive alternatives in an imaginative way, using concrete images rather than abstract principles. Visions of alternative futures offer hope instead of despair, a sense of the possible rather than resignation to the inevitable. Doomsday scenarios can be self-fulfilling prophecies if they undercut attempts to change. Most movements of social reform started from utopian imagination, new images of the good life, vivid portrayals of what might be (35). It is the combination of education, crises, power, and vision, then, that might create a just, free, and sustainable world.

I have mentioned some contributions of the biblical tradition to such a global vision. Other religious traditions will also have distinctive contributions to make. Communications today enable people to be aware of what is going on around the world in a way that was not possible in previous history. There is not only a revolution of rising expectations; there is a new demand for global justice. Events dramatize our interdependence. World-wide economic crises or rises in oil prices leave no nation untouched. Global awareness will have to come from many sources.

As a symbol of such awareness, think of the pictures of the earth that were taken by astronauts on the moon. For the first time, the earth could actually be seen as a single unit. There it is, a spinning globe of incredible richness and beauty, a blue and white gem among the barren planets. It has been proposed that we should think of it as Spaceship Earth (36). The earth is a fragile life-support system. Like a spaceship, it has limited resources that must be conserved and recycled. Its inhabitants are interdependent, sharing a mutual responsibility and a common destiny. This is a striking image that forcefully represents the importance of life-support and cooperation for human survival.

But we must extend the spaceship image if it is not to mislead us. A spaceship is a mechanical, man-made environment, devoid of life except for man. Planet earth, however, is enveloped in a marvelous web of life, a natural environment, of which humanity is a part and on which it is dependent. We must think not just of life-support but of ecological sustainability on a long time scale. So, too, the social order on a spaceship is relatively simple, with only a few people interacting in highly structured ways. On planet earth there are complex relationships between groups and nations, and there are issues of distributive justice and participatory freedom in the allocation of scarce resources. If freedom means participation in decision making, then globalism must be combined with localism and decentralization. As I see it, we must move toward globalism, and more localism, but less nationalism.

Let us keep before us that image of the spinning globe, but let us imagine its natural environments and its social order. The goal we seek is a just, free, and sustainable society on planet earth.

REFERENCES

1.   Meadows, D. H., et al. 1972. The Limits to Growth. Universe, New York.

2. Kahn, H., et al. (eds.). 1976. The Next 200 Years. William Morrow, New York.

3. Brown, L. 1978. The Twenty-Ninth Day. W. W. Norton & Company, Inc., New York. (A more optimistic appraisal is given in reference 4.)

4. Wortman, S., and Cummings, R. 1978. To Feed the World. Johns Hopkins University Press, Baltimore.

5. Barbour, I. G. (ed.). 1976. Finite Resources and the Human Future. Augsburg Press, Minneapolis.

6. Barbour, I. G. 1980. Technology, Environment and Human Values. Praeger Publishers, New York.

7. McNamara, R. 1974. The Third World: Millions face risk of death. Vital Speeches 41:12.

8. Lazlo, E. (ed.). 1977. Goals for Mankind, p. 275. E. P. Dutton & Company, Inc., New York.

9. Lappé, F. M. 1975. Diet for a Small Planet, Rev. Ed. Ballantine Books, Inc., New York.

10. Lappé, F. M., and Collins, J. 1977. Food First. Houghton Mifflin Company, Boston.

11. Erb, G., and Kallab, V. (eds.). 1975. Beyond Dependency: The Developing World Speaks Out. Praeger Publishers, New York.

12. ul Haq, M. 1976. The Poverty Curtain: Choices for the Third World. Columbia University Press, New York.

13. Simon, A. 1975. Bread for the World, p. 124. Eerdman's, Grand Rapids, Mich.

14. Rich, W. 1973. Smaller Families through Social and Economic Progress. Overseas Development Council, Washington, D.C.

15. Kocher, J. 1973. Rural Development, Income Distribution and Fertility Decline. Population Council, New York.

16. Ratcliffe, J. W. 1977. Poverty, politics and fertility: The anomaly of Kerala. Hastings Center Rep. 7:34–41.

17. Ophuls, W. 1977. Ecology and the Politics of Scarcity. W. H. Freeman & Company, San Francisco.

18. Heilbroner, R. 1974. An Inquiry into the Human Prospect. W. W. Norton & Company, Inc., New York.

19. Miles, R. 1976. Awakening from the American Dream: The Social and Political Limits to Growth. Universe, New York.

20. Leiss, W. 1976. The Limits of Satisfaction. University of Toronto Press, Toronto.

21. Center for Science in the Public Interest. 1977. 99 Ways to a Simple Lifestyle. Doubleday & Company, Inc., Garden City, N.Y.

22. Simple Living Collective, American Friends Service Committee. 1977. Taking Charge. Bantam Books, Inc., New York.

23. Gowan, S., et al. 1976. Moving Toward a New Society. New Society Press, Philadelphia.

24. Hayes, D. 1977. Rays of Hope: The Transition to a Post-Petroleum World. W. W. Norton & Company, Inc., New York.

25. Stanford Research Institute. 1977. Solar Energy in America's Future. U.S. Energy Research and Development Administration, Washington, D.C.

26. Lovins, A. 1976. Energy strategy: The road not taken? Foreign Affairs, October, pp. 65–96.

27. Cook, E. 1976. Man, Energy and Society. W. H. Freeman & Company, San Francisco.
28. Schipper, L., and Lichtenberger, A. 1976. Efficient energy use and well-being: The Swedish example. Science 194:1001–1013.
29. Tinbergen, J. (ed.). 1976. Reshaping the International Order, E. P. Dutton & Company, Inc., New York.
30. Birch, C. 1976. Creation, technology, and human survival. Ecumenical Rev., January.
31. Barbour, I. G. (ed.). 1973. Western Man and Environmental Ethics. Addison-Wesley Publishing Company, Inc., Reading, Mass.
32. Taylor, J. 1977. Enough is Enough. Augsburg Press, Minneapolis.
33. Birch, B., and Rasmussen, L. 1978. The Predicament of the Prosperous. Westminster Press, Philadelphia.
34. The Shakertown Pledge. In: Center for Science in the Public Interest. 1977. 99 Ways to a Simple Lifestyle. Doubleday & Company, Inc., Garden City, N.Y.
35. Bundy, R. (ed.). 1976. Images of the Future. Prometheus Books, Buffalo, N.Y.
36. Ward, B. 1966. Spaceship Earth. Columbia University Press, New York.

Index